"As a mom, I must have asked over a thousand times, 'Do I really have what it takes to raise my kids the right way?' And when I wasn't asking that, I was praying, 'Lord, help me!' That's why I'm so thrilled my dear friend Renee Swope has poured her godly and well-earned mothering wisdom into this beautiful book. It will help moms release the anxiety and shame that often weigh over-whelmed parents down. And even better, this message will build them up with the kind of hope and encouragement moms desper-ately need. The truths and help within the pages of *A Confident Mom* are timeless. Be sure to get your copy and let it transform your mom life today!"

Lysa TerKeurst, #1 *New York Times* bestselling author
and president of Proverbs 31 Ministries

"Renee's words are a guiding light wherever you are in mother-hood. Whether you're just starting your journey to motherhood or are several years in, *A Confident Mom* is filled with wisdom, encouragement, and practical ideas that will meet you right where you are and lift you up with everything you didn't even know you needed! Renee's voice is one you can trust, coming from a heart that has lived and is still living the truths written on each page."

Jordan Lee Dooley, national bestselling author
of *Own Your Everyday* and founder of Soul Scripts

"This book! Can you hear the cheering outside of your window? That would be me—and every woman reading these pages! Prac-tical and poignant, *A Confident Mom* is the book we've all been craving. Get ready to take a deep breath of relief as you devour Renee's words—relief that motherhood doesn't have to be perfect to be meaningful and relief that God's grace is a very real thing. From this book's application of biblical truth for all of our needs to its tactical solutions for changing our actions and attitudes, I cannot wait to read it again and again!"

Lara Casey, mom of three, author of *Cultivate* and *Make It
Happen*, and founder and CEO of Cultivate What Matters

"*A Confident Mom* is exactly the book every young mama needs to read. Every page brims with wisdom, honesty, and heartfelt encouragement from Renee as she shares her own story of mother-hood's struggles, triumphs, and joys—all while looking to Jesus. Renee writes as a mentor and friend on whom you can rely to de-velop the Lord's character w   ne time God is developing His   . I

am so thankful Renee took the time to write *A Confident Mom* and share it with such wisdom and tenderness. This is a must-read I will reference throughout my boy's growing up years!"

Gretchen Saffles, author of *The Well-Watered Woman* and the *Give Me Jesus* journal and founder of Well-Watered Women

"This book is a must-read for any mom whose thoughts move faster than her feet as she worries and wonders if she's doing enough and is enough for her kids. Renee speaks beautifully and powerfully to moms about God's unfolding grace and unfailing love, offering wisdom and simple ways to give your children what they need most! Within each truth-filled page of *A Confident Mom*, you'll find a friend who offers encouragement and practical tools to help you dissipate your doubts and gain unwavering confidence, knowing you are valued, more than enough, and so very loved as a mom and as a child of God."

Cindy Bultema, executive director of GEMS Girls' Clubs, speaker, and author of *Live Full Walk Free: Set Apart in a Sin-Soaked World* and *Red Hot Faith*

"Like a hand reaching out with hope and help, Renee's personal stories, confessions, revelations, and everyday life illustrations are for moms of every age and stage who long to lead and love their children with confidence. As I read her words, it felt like Renee was sitting with me, encouraging me like she has so many times before. I'm so excited for *A Confident Mom* to go out into the world to impact the lives of so many mamas who are desperate to hear truth and receive grace! This book will leave you inspired with simple and practical ideas and exhaling with sighs of relief while smiling as you discover grace and the God who gives and gifts it so freely."

Rachel Kang, author and founder of Indelible Ink Writers

"If you ever struggle with feelings of inadequacy and overwhelming responsibility as a parent, then *A Confident Mom* is just what you need! Renee throws a life preserver of hope to every mom who wants to parent well but doesn't have the tools to do so. Filled with timeless biblical truths, perspective-changing encouragement, and practical ideas for everyday parenting, this book will equip you to love your family in a way that honors God and nurtures relationships for the long haul!"

Krista Gilbert, home coach, author of *Reclaiming Home*, and cohost of *The Open Door Sisterhood* podcast

a confident mom

a confident mom

Simple Ways to Give Your Child

What They Need Most

Renee Swope

Revell

a division of Baker Publishing Group
Grand Rapids, Michigan

Published by Revell
a division of Baker Publishing Group
PO Box 6287, Grand Rapids, MI 49516-6287
www.revellbooks.com

Printed in the United States of America

Library of Congress Cataloging-in-Publication Data
Names: Swope, Renee, 1967– author.
Title: A confident mom : simple ways to give your child what they need most / Renee Swope.
Description: Grand Rapids, Michigan : Revell, a division of Baker Publishing Group, 2021. | Includes bibliographical references
Identifiers: LCCN 2020056319 | ISBN 9780800740771 (casebound) | ISBN 9780800738853 (paperback) | ISBN 9781493426690 (ebook)
Subjects: LCSH: Motherhood—Religious aspects—Christianity. | Motherhood—Biblical teaching. | Mothers—Religious life.
Classification: LCC BV4529.18 .S96 2021 | DDC 248.8/431—dc23
LC record available at https://lccn.loc.gov/2020056319

22   23   24   25   26   27   28   7   6   5   4   3   2   1

To Joshua and Andrew
Brandi and Hannah Rose

These pages hold some of the most
important parts of our family's story
and the legacy of our faith.
Thank you for your overwhelming support
and enthusiasm when I asked you guys
if I should write this book, and
the way you encouraged and prayed
for me while I did!

I dedicate this book to you and your children,
and your children's children.
Now that it's written, may I have
some grandbabies, please?

Let this be written for a future generation,
that a people not yet created may praise the LORD.

PSALM 102:18

contents

Contents

Part 3 What Your Heart Needs to Know

Part One

It Starts in Your Heart

one

The Day I Almost Quit

Before we get started, I think you need to know something. I really love my kids, but I have not always loved or even *liked* being a mom. When my baby boys turned into toddlers who wouldn't listen, I panicked inside. All my mom-friends looked like they knew what they were doing. Secretly, I wondered, *What is wrong with me? Why can't I figure out how to be a good mom?*

I was young, and my expectations were high. And I had a bad habit of comparing how I felt like a failure inside with other moms who looked like they had it all together on the outside. Whether I was at the park or the store, at church or a birthday party, it seemed like all the other moms knew what they were doing. Their children listened to them, and some moms even dressed their kids in matching outfits. I wondered how in the world they pulled it off. I could barely get a shower, get my kids dressed, and get us out of the house before lunch. It was easy to assume these other moms were killing it at motherhood, when in reality they were probably struggling and doubting themselves just like I was.

One afternoon, I filled my journal with scribbled words, guilt-ridden thoughts, tears, and desperate prayers. It had been a hard day, running too many errands with two small children. My to-do list included the dry cleaner, the pharmacy, the grocery store, and Target. By the time we got to our last stop, my boys were ready to climb monkey bars on a playground.

My two-year-old was fussy and tired. My four-year-old was being difficult. No matter how many times I told him, "I am not buying you any toys," he wouldn't stop asking. When I threatened him with consequences, he smiled and walked quietly beside me—for about sixty seconds. Then he started climbing in and out of the shopping cart to entertain himself and to annoy his little brother.

The last thing I needed was a store clerk to come around the corner and reprimand me for letting my kid break the safety rules. *Forget it!* I thought. Making a U-turn in the aisle, I headed to the checkout and wondered if maybe the cashier knew at what age kids learned to be content. *Maybe she'll tell me this is just a stage and he'll grow out of it*, I thought.

The checkout line led to more begging for pocket-sized toys and candy bars strategically placed at eye-level for small children. Could it get any worse? I opted out of asking the cashier for parenting advice, unloaded my stuff onto the checkout conveyor belt as fast as I could, and left the store as quickly as possible.

On the drive home, I made sure Joshua knew just how frustrated I was with him. I told him that because he wouldn't listen, both he and Andrew were going to eat lunch and take an early nap when we got home. No playtime. No snuggles. No stories. No songs. I was done!

After the boys ate lunch and went down for their naps, I started thinking how I could convince my husband to fire me. It wasn't that I wanted to actually quit being a mom (although I'm sure I felt that way some days). I just wanted to quit doing the hard parts of parenting while working part-time and staying home with our boys.

I thought if I could go back to working full-time, at least I would be with people who appreciated my efforts and listened to me (most of the time). And maybe someone else could teach my kids how to be kind, patient, obedient, and content.

I had a feeling my husband wouldn't agree to firing me, so I decided to look for some pink construction paper and write "I QUIT!" on it. That way I could turn in my pink slip when he got home. Unfortunately, all of our pink construction paper was gone. It was definitely not turning out to be my best day.

Normally, I would make a cup of coffee, start a load of laundry, and enjoy some quiet while the boys napped, but not that day. I decided I needed to do something that would make me feel competent and like I'd accomplished something that day.

Reaching into my work bag, I pulled out an article my friend Lysa had asked me to edit. I shook my head and sighed as I read the title: "Bringing Out the Winner in Your Child." It seemed like I couldn't avoid the topic, no matter how hard I tried.

A few paragraphs into Lysa's article, she referenced *Raising Positive Kids in a Negative World*, where author Zig Ziglar shares a story about Andrew Carnegie. Carnegie was the wealthiest man in America in the early 1900s, and at one point he was so successful he employed more than forty-three millionaires, which was unheard of at the time. Intrigued by his wealth, a reporter asked Carnegie how he had hired forty-three millionaires. Andrew Carnegie explained that

> the men were not millionaires when they started working for him but had become millionaires as a result. The reporter then asked, "How did you develop these men to become so valuable to you that you have paid them this much money?"
>
> "Men are developed the same way gold is mined," Carnegie explained. "When gold is mined, several tons of dirt must be moved to get an ounce of gold, but one doesn't go into the mine looking for dirt, one goes in looking for gold, and the more he looks for the more he finds."[1]

Ziglar used this story to encourage parents to "look for the gold in their children instead of focusing on their faults."[2] Gold? What gold? I didn't see any. Not even a speck. All I saw was the dirt of my child's disobedience and discontent along with my defeated mindset and critical attitude.

I felt like such a failure. And I was sure God was just as disappointed in me as I was in myself. The critical words I said to Joshua on the way home replayed in my head. I cringed as I thought about the harsh tone of my voice as I intentionally tried to make my son feel guilty for his behavior. It wasn't my best parenting moment for sure.

I didn't feel like editing anymore, so I put my work down and pulled out my journal. Filling blank pages with scribbled thoughts, I wrote,

> I hate who I have become. I'm such a horrible mom. Why didn't someone tell me how hard this was going to be? I'm frustrated with my kids and myself. I have no patience and I don't know what I am doing! I feel guilty all the time. I couldn't wait to be a mom and now I want to quit. I wish I had a gold miner in my life who could see something good in me.[3]

This was not the first time I felt like a failure as a mom, and I knew it wouldn't be the last. I wished there was someone I could talk to. Sadly, I was too ashamed to tell any of my friends how much I was struggling because I was afraid they might judge me.

As you hold this book in your hands, I wonder how many really hard days you've had as a mom. Maybe you've compared yourself to other moms and felt like a failure too. Or you've had expectations of yourself and your kids that have created a world of disappointment. I wonder if you feel alone in your doubts and discouragement, like I did. Maybe you don't think you have what it takes to be a good mom, and you're afraid your inadequacies and failures will cause your kids to need a therapist or stop them from following God. I know just how you feel, and so does almost every other mom.

What you need is someone to help you process your thoughts and buried hopes, your doubts and high expectations. Someone who will show you how to depend on God's Word as your foundation and His love as your guide. Someone who will help you discover simple ways to give your children what they need most while letting God give you what your heart needs most from Him.

You see, when I set out to accomplish something that afternoon, I had no idea what God was about to accomplish in me as He began to change my perspective as a mom and encourage my heart as a child of God.

As the Lord helped me grasp how He parented me, it changed the way I parented my children. In the days and years that followed, God shifted my focus away from correcting my kids' habits to connecting with their hearts. Instead of me always noticing their shortcomings, He showed me how to notice and nurture their character. Over the past twenty years God has helped me understand His grace through relationship-driven parenting while releasing me from the burden of performance-based living.

I had no idea what God was about to accomplish in me as He began to change my perspective as a mom and encourage my heart as a child of God.

Those little boys who were two and four are now twenty-three and twenty-six, and both are married. We also have a twelve-year-old daughter, Aster, who our family adopted from Ethiopia when she was ten months old. I've gone before you, and I'm still right there with you in the trenches of motherhood, leaning on God's grace and everything He taught me the day I almost quit and in the years that followed.

This is the story of His unfolding grace and unfailing love that helped me see that everything I needed to know as a mom, I would learn as a child of God.

Everything I needed to know as a mom, I would learn as a child of God.

If you long for encouragement and hope, along with practical tools and biblical truths to help you become a confident mom, I'd love to be that someone for you I wish I'd had so many years ago.

Lord, thank You for seeing me and knowing what I need. Thank You for coming to my rescue on the days when my mom-doubts and discouragement make me question if I'm doing anything right. I need Your perspective and encouragement. I need Your help to process my thoughts and hopes, my doubts and dreams, my desires and expectations. Show me simple ways to give my children what they need most while making space and time for You to give me what my heart needs most from You. Amen.

two

Finding a
New Place to Start

As I poured out my heart in my journal that day, I wrote down everything I was thinking. It was painful to read my own words, but it was important for me to see what was going on in my heart.

And just as I finished writing "I couldn't wait to be a mom and now I want to quit. I wish I had a gold miner in my life who could see something good in me," I sensed God whispering to my heart, *Renee, I am that gold miner. You are the one who is so critical of yourself. You are the one who focuses on your mistakes and beats yourself up with accusation and condemnation. Those are not My thoughts. I see the gold of My image, woven into your heart when I created you. And I want to bring it to the surface so your kids can see it too.*

Have you ever sensed God whispering something to your heart or leading your thoughts in a direction that is not normal for you? His voice is not audible to your ears but is clear inside your mind,

21

like the words are rising up from inside you. That's what was happening to me. The possibility that God wasn't focused on my faults gave me a sense of hope, but I questioned if it was just my thoughts or really His Spirit encouraging me. I couldn't imagine how God saw anything good in me that day.

I decided to take what I sensed God was saying and compare it to Scripture to see if it was consistent with His Word and His character. I remembered times in Scripture when God didn't let someone's failure or inadequacy define them or hold them back from being used by Him. Times when Jesus extended grace and mercy to people who were a mess, just like me.

As those stories came to mind, I opened the pages of my Bible to find them. First, I turned to Judges 6 to read about Gideon, a man who hid from his enemies in a winepress—until God called him a mighty warrior and helped him become one. God told Gideon to go in the strength he had and not focus on what he didn't have. Just like Andrew Carnegie developed those men to reach their fullest potential, God saw beyond who Gideon was to who he could become.

I also thought about Moses, a man who struggled with self-doubt and insecurity. His story begins in the book of Exodus. When God called Moses to be His mouthpiece and lead His people out of Egypt, Moses listed all the reasons he was not a good choice. But God didn't give up on him. With His presence and help, Moses became what God called and created him to be. Did he do it perfectly? Nope. But God didn't focus on Moses's faults or failures. He focused on Moses's desire to be faithful and his willingness to trust God with his whole heart.

With each story I read, I sensed God confirming He saw beyond who I was to who I could become. The day I wanted to quit was the day I started to realize how destructive my critical thoughts were and how much I had allowed self-doubt, inadequacy, shame, and guilt to define me. And all of it was destroying my confidence and joy as a mom.

But God was there with me that day—in the store, at the cash register, in the car on the way home, at the table as I rushed the boys through lunch and hurried them to their beds. He saw my heart unraveling in frustration and defeat. And He was there waiting for me to sit down so He could show me I didn't have to stay in this hard place. I didn't need to quit; I just needed a new place to start.

> I didn't need to quit; I just needed a new place to start.

Deconstructing the Lies of Performance-Based Living

Although I loved the concept of becoming like a gold miner, I knew it would be hard for me to see the good in my children if all I saw were flaws in myself. So, I decided to pursue an understanding of both. I asked God to show me what the gold would look like in my kids and what was going on inside of me. Why did I feel driven to get so much done that day and every other day? And why was I constantly berating myself with criticism and comparison?

His answers didn't come in a day or even in a week. They came over time as I journaled and prayed, read through the Psalms and the Gospels, and listened to worship songs. I remember praying Psalm 25:4–5, "Show me your ways, LORD, teach me your paths. Guide me in your truth and teach me, for you are God my Savior, and my hope is in you all day long." And He did.

One day, while I was journaling, I had a flashback from college. In it, I was sitting on the floor in my apartment talking on the phone with my mom, who was three hours away. With tears pouring down my cheeks, I choked out the most vulnerable questions I had ever asked: "Mom, will you still love me if I never accomplish anything ever again? If I don't make the dean's list, or graduate with honors, or get a great job offer, or finish college . . . will you still love me?" I was in the middle of an emotional breakdown and everything I had been thinking and feeling for years just came pouring out.

When that memory came out of nowhere, I sensed God was showing me how things from my childhood had impacted my perspective and approach to motherhood, and that looking back would help me move forward.

Growing up, I remember longing for more of my mom's time and attention. My parents were divorced, and my two brothers and I lived with our mom, who worked long hours, late nights, and many weekends. When she wasn't at work, she was busy doing other things or having a drink with friends. I didn't realize it, but I must have believed her lack of availability meant I wasn't worth her time. Like a little sponge, I soaked up the details of how Mom spent her money, her time, and her attention, believing if I pursued the things she valued, she would value me.

From middle school through college, I worked multiple jobs and participated in more extracurricular activities than should have been allowed. If I was earning money and doing something significant, it felt like I mattered.

I also felt like I was running a race that didn't have a finish line, always trying to catch my breath but afraid to slow down. When I was sixteen, I started struggling with anxiety and depression. Instead of cutting back, I kept pushing myself. And my mom encouraged it because she thought being busy would distract me or make me happy, because she didn't know any better. By my junior year in college, I had almost everything I wanted, yet I felt like I had nothing.

Depleted, hopeless, and chronically fatigued, I couldn't keep going. All my doing came to a screeching halt. My capacity collapsed. Sadly, when I could no longer be productive as a high achiever, I felt worthless and unworthy of love. And I think that's why I asked Mom if she would still love me if I never accomplished another thing. "Of course I will still love you, Renee," she assured me, and begged me to come home.

Our Worth Is Not Determined by Our Work

When we believe our worth is determined by our work, whether in an office or at home, volunteer or paid, the thought of slowing down is terrifying. Some of us grew up in families or churches that influenced our beliefs about our worth. But these aren't the only influences. We live in a culture filled with messaging that tells us our productivity proves our worth. And it is a lie from the pit of hell that is wreaking havoc on our mental health, our physical and spiritual well-being, our youth, and our families. We have got to recognize this underlying belief that has too much power and influence over our decisions and in the direction of our lives.

If we are going to become confident moms in Christ and live in the fullness of God's will for us and our families, we have got to take hold of our thoughts and our time. And we have to give God full access to rewire both around this truth: our value has been predetermined by the One who made us, and it is firmly established in the unshakable power and permanence of God's unconditional love.

> Our value has been predetermined by the One who made us, and it is firmly established in the unshakable power and permanence of God's unconditional love.

This is the truth that rescued me from my downward spiral, a few weeks after my breakdown, when I'd returned to finish classes and decided to visit a church near my college campus. They "happened" to be doing a sermon series about God's unconditional love. Honestly, I didn't know unconditional love was even possible. I had never seen those two words next to each other in a sentence. But through those messages, God answered so many of my questions and set me on a journey of seeking and finding the love I had been looking for.

25

When I became a mom, I unknowingly fell back into my old thought patterns of performance-based living. And here I was, married and a mama of two, remembering how much I had forgotten. Like the first time God told me He loved me while I was reading one of my favorite books, *Longing for Love*. In it, the author referenced Isaiah 43, so I opened my Bible and read, "Fear not, for I have redeemed you; I have called you by name, you are mine. . . . Because *you are precious in my eyes*, and honored, and *I love you*" (vv. 1, 4 ESV, emphasis added).

It says I love you, I thought to myself. *God actually says I love you.*

Do you need to hear those words of assurance like I did thirty years ago and every day that followed? I especially needed to hear them the day I found myself running again. Running myself ragged as I ran too many errands with my two little boys.

God wants to say those words to you today. *I love you. You don't have to "do" anything to make Me love you more. You are Mine. And you are enough, just as you are.*

Lord, I need a new place to start, a place where I can slow down long enough to let You love me. A place where I can be reminded that my worth is not based on my work. Your unconditional love bestows value on me that I could never earn. Thank You for loving me and for seeing beyond my flaws and failures. Help me start over by remembering who I am as Your child so I can become who You created me to be as a mom. Amen.

three

Reorienting Your Heart to the Goodness of God

Has shame ever made you feel like you are the only one who struggles? You have an enemy who will use your doubts and discouragement, comparison and self-criticism to isolate you and bombard you with a list of your flaws and failures. His goal is to get you so consumed by discouragement and doubt that you'll feel too tired and ashamed to go to Jesus with them.

In our self-rejection, it's easy to assume God's opinion of us is the same as our opinion of ourselves. I was convinced God was as disappointed in me as I was in myself the day I wanted to quit. But my assumption about God's thoughts toward me couldn't have been further from the truth. The same unconditional love that captivated my heart years before was there to set me free from condemnation that day.

If I had remembered the goodness of God's grace and forgiveness, I would have run to Him instead of trying to run away from

Him and my role as a mom. If only I had remembered the words of King David: "The Lord is gracious and compassionate, slow to anger and rich in love. The LORD is good to all; he has compassion on all he has made" (Ps. 145:8–9).

Knowing God's Heart toward Us

Our understanding of God's heart in adulthood is influenced by the image we had of Him in our childhood. When I was growing up, God seemed distant and invisible. He lived at church but not in our home. I remember walking through the motions of tradition but having no concept of who He was or His heart toward me.

There was a crucifix at the front of our church that made me sad when I looked at it. It was depressing and confusing to me that a church would hang such a painful reminder of an innocent man killed by cruel people. I had no idea Jesus was the Son of God. I did not know the cross was not there to remind me of people's cruelty but to tell me again and again of God's love.

Our understanding of God's heart in adulthood is influenced by the image we had of Him in our childhood.

Throughout my childhood the distance between us grew less and less, but God was still invisible to me. Then, in college, I came to know God through the person of Jesus, "the radiance of God's glory and the exact representation of his being" (Heb. 1:3). The apostle John describes how God put skin on and came to be with us. He takes us back to the commencement of time and tells us, "In the beginning was the Word . . . [and] the Word became flesh and made his dwelling among us" (John 1:1, 14). Through Jesus, God's invisible character becomes visible to us.

Jesus told His disciples, "Anyone who has seen me has seen the Father" (14:9). As I began to understand how much I needed to know God's heart so that He could change my perspective of myself and of Him, I knew I needed to spend more time with Jesus, getting to know Him more intimately.

When you spend time with Jesus, you get to know the heart of your heavenly Father through reflections of Him in His Son. I want us to look at some important snapshots of Jesus's life together, searching for the image of our Father in His Son. I want you to see how He loves you through all that He's offered others, because it's what He offers you today.

He Is Available

When you leave to go on a long trip, what is the last thing you say to those you are leaving? "I love you." "Call me." "Feed the dog." You say what you want them to remember, and Jesus did the same. Jesus's last words to the disciples were, "I am with you always, to the very end" (Matt. 28:20).

Jesus had lived those words, and now they were His final reminder. Unless He needed to pull away to be with the Father, He was there for those who loved Him and those He loved.

Jesus skipped lunch one day to talk with a Samaritan woman. Afterward, she went home to tell everyone about Him. But knowing *about* Him wasn't enough. They wanted to *know* Him.

> [So] they urged him to stay with them, and he stayed two days. And because of his words many more became believers. They said to the woman, "We no longer believe just because of what you said; now we have heard for ourselves, and we know this man really is the Savior of the world." (John 4:40–42)

They got to know Him because He was available to be with them.

Jesus didn't see requests for His time as interruptions, but instead welcomed them as invitations. He slowed down to share His heart and to listen to their questions. He knew time spent with

29

people would give them insight into who they were and what they were searching for.

We need to know God is always available for us. He wants us to come to Him regularly, not just on Sunday or while we are reading our Bibles. He wants to be with us and be there for us all throughout our day. Whether we talk, laugh, cry, or be quiet, Jesus loves hanging out with us. No matter how much or how little we need, He is always available.

He Is Approachable

Not only is Jesus available, but He is approachable as well. Lepers, prostitutes, tax collectors, men, women, and children—all drew near to Jesus and He drew near to them. Although most religious leaders of the time had a demeanor that pushed people away, "Jesus had a differentness that drew people to Him. He was the most approachable person they had ever seen."[1] One of the most unusual things about Jesus's approachability is that He was a rabbi. In that day, a rabbi's role was to make sure people were following the religious law.

The law stated no one could touch a leper, so lepers were kept outside the city gates. To make sure no one came near them, people with leprosy had to shout, "Unclean, unclean." Lepers avoided all people, but especially rabbis, because they'd get in trouble for breaking the law if they got too close to a rabbi.

One day while Jesus was walking down the street, a man covered in leprosy saw Jesus and "begged him, 'Lord, if you are willing, you can make me clean.'" Overwhelmed with compassion, "Jesus reached out his hand and touched the man. 'I am willing,' he said. 'Be clean!' And immediately the leprosy left him" (Luke 5:12–13).

He's approachable and He's willing—He extends His hand to touch and be touched even when we feel unworthy or untouchable.

Do you ever struggle to believe God is approachable or that you are worth His time and attention? If so, tell Him and ask Jesus to help you get to know Him better. Spend time reading the book of John and highlight every time you see evidence of Jesus's unique approachability and His willingness to draw near to those who were avoided by others. No matter how many times you fail, He will still be there with open arms, waiting to touch your heart and restore your hope.

He Is Aware

The Bible tells us God knows when we sit and when we rise. He knows our thoughts. He discerns when we go and when we lie down; He is familiar with all our ways (Ps. 139:2–3). Most of us wonder if we have even been noticed. God makes it clear we are the focus of His attention. He knows our every thought and need.

No matter who they were or what they wanted, Jesus was aware of and attentive to people's needs. Whether they were big or small, short or tall, He had tenderness to give to each one. People brought their loved ones to Him day and night. Sometimes the disciples would try to intercept what they saw as interruptions. They were especially hesitant when people brought babies to Jesus to have Him touch them. "When the disciples saw this, they rebuked them. But Jesus called the children to him and said, 'Let the little children come to me, and do not hinder them'" (Luke 18:15–16).

He wasn't only available for cute little kids with gap-toothed smiles. He was also aware of the needs of blind men, crippled old ladies, demon-possessed teenagers, and many others. In the book of Luke we see Jesus pausing to offer His attention to a

> Most of us wonder if we have even been noticed. God makes it clear we are the focus of His attention. He knows our every thought and need.

hemorrhaging woman (8:40–48). She did not even ask Him to stop, but He noticed when she touched His robe. Although He was on His way to heal a dying child, He stopped to meet this woman's needs. There is never a time when He isn't aware or when our needs aren't important to Him.

Jesus didn't expect a list of credentials from the people who came to Him, but He did have some requirements. They had to come with hands open to release things they held on to so they could receive the healing and hope He offered. They had to come with hearts willing to let go of the past and all that hindered them from the future He promised and be willing to embrace the truth of His grace and forgiveness so they could live in the security of His love. Are your hands open? Is your heart willing?

Jesus was available and gave His time. He was approachable and gave His touch. He was attentive and gave His tenderness. Just like the Samaritans, the more time we spend with Him, looking for evidence of how He loves and lives, the more we experience His presence and His love in a way we never have before. We won't only know *about* Him; we will *know* Him.

Lord, I want to know the truth about who You are and the truth about who I am as Your child. Remind me that You are always available, approachable, and attentive to my needs. I lay down any misconceptions or misunderstandings I have about You and ask that You would help me come to know You and experience the truth of who You are in a way I never have before. Please give me a better understanding of my role as Your child and my role as a parent. I want to know You and become more like You, so my children will see You in me. Amen.

four

Turning Self-Defeat into Self-Awareness

I was tired of struggling with comparison, discontent, and my cruel inner critic. I wanted things to change, and it was becoming clear that I had to make changes and be willing to change. But I didn't know what changes were needed until I got brave enough to ask Jesus to show me. I started asking Him to help me turn my self-defeat into self-awareness whenever I found myself in a downward spiral.

As I became more self-aware and secure in the fact that God loves me unconditionally and wants my best, I decided to borrow King David's vulnerable and courageous prayer: "Search me, O God, and know my heart; test my thoughts. Point out anything you find in me that makes you sad, and lead me along the path of everlasting life" (Ps. 139:23–24 TLB).

Praying these words was my way of inviting God into the process of examining my thoughts, emotions, and actions to see if there were any patterns causing me to sabotage my joy and purpose, especially as a mom. And I discovered that God is gracious and willing to give us wisdom and clarity when we ask Him for it (Prov. 2:6; James 1:5).

Owning My Part

As I distanced myself emotionally from what happened, I could see the facts of how I had set myself up for failure by planning a day filled with striving and fueled by my drive to get things done. My internal comparisons to other moms had triggered feelings of never being or doing enough. Those thoughts and behavior patterns left me empty and frustrated, filled with self-doubt and horrible discouragement.

I craved the satisfaction of completing my long to-do list. I also wanted to get my errands run while Joshua was not in preschool so I would have extra time to get more done at home and work while Joshua was in preschool the next day. However, the reason we had him in preschool was to give me three mornings a week for work time, project time, and me time.

I pushed my kids and myself to do too much in too little time. I even tried to convince myself running errands could be like a "field trip" to the drugstore, the grocery store, the dry cleaner, and Target. Checking those errands off my list gave me a sense of purpose and worth. And that's where I went off the rails. I had attached my value to what I could get done, and now I was coming undone.

I had attached my value to what I could get done, and now I was coming undone.

It was unrealistic for me to expect Joshua to not be wiggly and bored. What four-year-old likes to run errands with his mom? And why had I not sprinkled in a break at the playground or an ice cream shop to balance our day with something the boys would enjoy? Joshua was in preschool three mornings a

34

week. I'm sure he wanted to be at home playing with his brother or at the park for a playdate with a friend.

I had been frustrated with Joshua for not listening and not being content, and for getting on my nerves instead of going along with my plans. I also felt guilty for not being the kind of mom who magically organized her life in such a way that all her laundry was done and her errands completed on Saturday morning before her children woke up. And I was ashamed of myself for wanting to quit the hard parts of parenting.

Making Adjustments

One of the things I learned the hard way is that when I am having a super stressful day, I need to stop and evaluate what I'm doing and why I'm doing it. Pausing my agenda long enough to ask myself if something needs to be adjusted in our schedule or if I need to pivot my plans to make things better—for myself and my kids—is always a good idea. I also need to ask myself what my children are capable of at their age and with their unique wiring, and build in consideration for what will set them and me up for success.

That comes from a place of love—a place of loving my kids and loving myself enough to want things to go well and to want our day to be a positive experience for us all. This is a much better place than plowing through our day, fueled by my desire to knock out my to-do list and get errands run so I could enjoy my free time the next day. Now, I'm not saying that needing and enjoying free time is wrong. It is absolutely good and beautiful, but when it causes my kids and me to experience super high levels of stress that lead to me losing my temper and wanting to call it quits, something needs to be adjusted.

In Retrospect

I have good days and bad days when it comes to doing the wisest thing in the moment. Now, after a series of hard days or situations,

I have learned to block out time to sit with Jesus and ask Him to help me do what my husband calls a "retrospective" to identify where things got off track so I can gain wisdom and self-awareness. Here are some questions I ask myself.

Expectations

1. What were my expectations?
2. What did not go the way I hoped it would? What did?
3. Did I leave margin for the unexpected? Was it enough?
4. Did I communicate my expectations to my children (if age appropriate)?
5. Were my expectations realistic or unrealistic based on my kids' ages and eating and sleep schedule?
6. Did anything happen to throw our schedule off that I didn't make adjustments for because I didn't want to change my plans?

Behavior Patterns

1. What time of day was it?
2. What happened right before things went downhill?
3. Was I on my phone, ignoring my children, or pulled in multiple directions?
4. Is there a pattern I can see when I compare today to other bad days?
5. Were my children tired, hungry, not feeling great, bored, antsy, or craving attention?
6. What about me? Was I hungry, tired, or not feeling great?
7. Is there a behavior I need to change (e.g., calls, hurry, scheduling overload)?
8. Is there something I could have done differently to set my kids and myself up for a better experience together?

With Jesus by Our Side

Healthy self-awareness is crucial to becoming a confident mom, but we need to recognize the risk of self-defeat and ask these questions with Jesus by our side. One thing that helps me prepare my heart and my thoughts is reading and praying Scriptures like these:

> For the LORD gives wisdom;
> From His mouth come knowledge and understanding.
> (Prov. 2:6 NASB)

> Sincerity and truth are what you require;
> fill my mind with your wisdom. (Ps. 51:6 GNT)

I also ask the Lord to give me wisdom and clarity and to silence condemnation and confusion. Then I write down a condensed version of these questions in my journal with my answers. When we write things down, we are more likely to find out what is going on inside us by looking at our feelings and the facts.

It is also extremely helpful to see it all on paper instead of it being jumbled in our heads. Seeing it on paper is the only way I can look at what I'm doing and notice if there are things I need to change or factors I need to consider.

I also date that page in my journal and write "retrospective—see journal" on my calendar so I can easily find it later in my journal based on the date. Being able to compare days like these over a period of time helps me notice patterns in my behavior and in my kids' behaviors.

Unrealistic expectations, mom-guilt, self-shaming, and doubt, plus an accumulation of comparisons, fueled my cruel inner critic; it all got the best of me, and my kids got the worst of me. But eventually I was able to make the best of a bad situation by learning and growing from it.

Bad Days Don't Make You a Bad Mom

You are going to have bad days, but they do not make you a bad mom. They can actually help make you a wise mom. When you start sinking in self-defeat, turn it into self-awareness by taking time to look at the facts and learn from them, without labeling yourself for them.

And on those days when your inner critic gets loud and mean, take that wisdom and self-awareness you are gaining to a whole new level by comparing what you are saying to yourself with what God's Word says in response.

When You Say . . .	God's Word Says*
No matter how hard I try, it's never enough.	The humble will see their God at work and be glad. Let all who seek God's help be encouraged. Psalm 69:32 NLT
I'm such a bad mom.	Your statutes are wonderful; therefore I obey them. The unfolding of your words gives light; it gives understanding to the simple. Psalm 119:129–30
I can't stop doubting my parenting decisions.	For the LORD will be your confidence, and will keep your foot from being caught. Proverbs 3:26 NASB

Lord, thank You for showing me I don't have to live in a cycle of self-defeat. By Your grace I can learn from my mistakes and stop labeling myself for them. Remind me to slow down to ask myself good questions and make adjustments to set myself and my children up for success. I want to embrace the wisdom of living an examined life before You. I invite You

*Excerpted from "What God's Word Says," which includes thirty of our most common mom-doubts and God's truths to help you replace discouraging things we say to ourselves with what God's Word says in response. Take a look on page 195 for extra encouragement as you keep reading.

to search me and know my heart, to examine my thoughts and show me anything in me that makes you sad. Lord, I want You to lead me and give me the courage to make wise choices and changes so that I can experience Your abundance in my life. Amen.

five

Becoming a Gold-Mining Mom

A s I mentioned in chapter 2, while I was asking the Lord to show me what was going on in my heart, I was also asking Him to show me what it would look like to become like a gold miner in my parenting mindset. That afternoon, while the boys were still napping and the house was still quiet, I decided to do a brain dump of ideas around the concept of mining for gold in the hearts of my children.

Adjusting My Focus

I thought about how gold miners focus on finding gold even though the main thing they see is dirt. I would need to adjust my focus, knowing that what I looked for would determine what I found.

As I sat there trying to figure out what the gold would look like, I thought about traits my husband, J.J., and I had talked about wanting to develop in our boys, like patience, kindness, thankfulness, and generosity. A few weeks before, we had tried to start a family devotion series focused on developing biblical character in kids, but Joshua wasn't interested.

Maybe the concept of mining for gold could move us in that direction from a different angle. As I wrote down a few character traits, my favorite verse from the creation story popped into my mind: "So God created human beings in his own image. In the image of God he created them; male and female he created them" (Gen. 1:27 NLT). I wrote that down too.

That verse reminded me of what I had written in my journal earlier, when I sensed God saying He saw the gold of His image woven into my heart when He created me. I wondered if I was supposed to mine for gold that looked like God. It sounded weird at first, but it also made sense that the gold in each of us would be a reflection of God's character, since we are created in His image. God's desire is for all of us to have hearts that look more and more like His.

At the top of my paper, I wrote "Golden Attitudes and Actions." Then I added more traits that reflected God's heart and His Word, like sharing, contentment, perseverance, courage, and responsibility.

When Joshua and Andrew woke up from their naps, I put my list aside and apologized to Joshua for being harsh with him. He gave me a hug and said he forgave me. About an hour later, J.J. came home from work, and after we got the kids to bed that night, I told him about everything that had happened, including my failed attempts at firing myself. He listened, encouraged me, and said he was willing to try whatever I came up with.

Gathering My Tools

I needed more than an idea in my head. I wanted a practical tool in my hands. I mean, gold miners need tools to help them find gold and bring it to the surface, so it made sense that I did too. The next day I decided to create 3 × 3 inch character trait cards on my computer. At the top of each card, I wrote the character trait in bold letters and added clip art under it that Joshua picked out to illustrate each trait. I also looked up Bible verses for each trait and thought about God's Word being "a lamp for my feet, a light on my path" (Ps. 119:105), just like a lamp on a gold miner's hardhat that illuminates his or her path in the darkness.

I needed more than an idea in my head. I wanted a practical tool in my hands.

Later that week, I bought posterboard and created a small chart to hang in our kitchen so I could display the character trait cards. Even though I still wasn't sure how this was going to play out, I just took the next step. I figured it would eventually all come together and I would have a system or at least a guided approach to help me see and seek God's best in my kids.

Changing My Lens

One Saturday our family packed up our SUV and headed to the soccer fields to watch Andrew play. My mom was with us and, as she walked behind me to the sideline where we were going to sit down, she said, "Renee, your hair is the strangest red color. Have you seen your hair?"

"Yes, I saw my hair in the mirror this morning, Mom," I told her.

"Well, you need to get your hairdresser to fix it!" she insisted.

Oh well, it's just Mom, I thought to myself and decided I was not going to let her comments hurt my feelings.

When we reached our spot beside the soccer field, I arranged my blanket on the ground and Mom sat behind me in a chair. I had barely sat down when she said, "Renee, your toenail polish is so orange. Why would you wear toenail polish that looks like that?"

I was now convinced Mom was going color blind and turned around to tell her. That's when I noticed she was wearing big auburn-colored sunglasses, which were causing her to see everything in bright shades of orange and red.

Like my mom's sunglasses, the lens we look through is like a filter that defines or distorts what we see. When we look through a lens of unrealistic expectations, we will see inadequacy and imperfection. When we look through a lens of comparison, we will see flaws and failure. When we look through a lens of impatience, we will see inconvenience and interruptions.

But when we look through a lens of faith, we will see promise and potential. When we look through a lens of hope, we will see progress and possibility. When we look through a lens of love, we will see beyond who our child is and believe in who they can become.

In 1 Samuel 16, God challenges the prophet Samuel to change his lens, which was focused on outward appearances, and put on a God-shaped lens that looks at the heart. God sent Samuel to find a new king, and when Samuel arrived at the home of Jesse and asked to see his sons, Jesse sent out his older sons, but he did not include his youngest son, David.

> When they arrived, Samuel saw Eliab and thought, "Surely the Lord's anointed stands here before the Lord."
> But the Lord said to Samuel, "Do not consider his appearance or his height, for I have rejected him. The Lord does not look at the things people look at. People look at the outward appearance, but the Lord looks at the heart." (1 Sam. 16:6–7)

The heart of God had the heart of David in mind for a king. Although his father didn't see potential in David, God knew it was there.

Andrew Carnegie was similar. Because he was committed to bringing out the best in the men who worked for him, he chose a lens that helped him see and develop their strengths instead of focusing on their weaknesses. As a result, he recognized their value and helped them reach their full potential.

When I intentionally chose to look for my boys to show good character, I was more likely to notice them carrying their plate to the kitchen without being asked or packing their book bag the night before school or remembering to feed the dog. With Jesus's help and a God-shaped lens, I started to see what I had been missing because I simply had not been looking for it.

Developing the Gold Within

One afternoon J.J. reminded me that our friend Michael, who was a geologist, might know something about gold that would be interesting or helpful. I decided to call Michael to see if there were any correlations between gold developing in the ground and character developing in our hearts.

When I asked Michael how gold is formed, he explained that it is developed in an open area of rock when the right chemicals come together in the right environment, under the right conditions of moisture and temperature. I expected it to be more complicated, but Michael basically broke it down into three simple parts.

With Jesus's help and a God-shaped lens, I started to see what I had been missing because I simply had not been looking for it.

After we hung up, I thought about the three things Michael had mentioned: the right ingredients (chemicals), in the right environment, under the right conditions. What if there was a way to not only discover gold but develop the gold of God's character in our children's hearts by providing the right ingredients, environment, and conditions?

I had a journal full of notes I'd taken over the years as I read Christian parenting books and listened to sermons, messages, and interviews about parenting. I noticed consistent themes that aligned with what God had been showing me about how He parents us. I spent time looking through my notes and asking Jesus to show me what I'd needed growing up and what my children needed now. Based on all of those notes, talking to other moms, and lots of prayer, here is where I landed:

> We can develop the gold of God's character in our children's hearts by offering them the **ingredients** of encouraging words, God's Word, and an emphasis on character in an **environment** of acceptance, approval, affirmation, and unconditional love under the **conditions** of heart connection, belonging, affirmation, listening, quality time, patience, awareness, an accurate portrayal of God's goodness and grace, fun and loving biblical discipline, the power of apology, and forgiveness.

Easy peasy, right? Just kidding. I know it is a lot, but I am excited and encouraged to tell you that you can do this! In part 2, we will unpack each of these important pieces and discover simple ways to give our children what they need most so they can become the best version of who God created them to be.

Lord, I want to see my kids the way You see them and love them the way You do. Help me adjust my focus to match Yours and change my lens so that I can see the heart of my child and what matters most. I want to be like a gold miner, willing to look past the dirt to discover and develop the gold of Your character in them. Remind me to not look for dirt but to look for gold, knowing the more I look for, the more I will find. Amen.

Part Two

What Your Child Needs Most

six

Your Child Needs to Know You Believe in Them

I can't!" Andrew shouted with tears streaming down his cheeks. I looked down and saw our Etch A Sketch next to him on the floor. Joshua, who is two-and-a-half years older, was trying to teach him how to use it, but Andrew was frustrated with those two little white knobs at the bottom of the hard red plastic frame and gave up before he barely even tried.

"I can't!" had been Andrew's response to every obstacle he'd faced that week. "I can't," he'd cried as I encouraged him to put his head underwater at the pool. "I can't," he'd muttered when I asked him to tell me the first letter in the word *airplane.* "I can't! I can't! I can't!"

I can't take it anymore! I thought to myself as I watched him sit in defeat. Then it dawned on me. Andrew had grown frustrated with himself while trying to do things his big brother could do well. He was stuck in the mud of "I can't" and trapped by the muck of comparison.

I empathized with Andrew's discouragement. How many times had I wanted to sit on the sidelines and watch others rather than try something difficult? Wondering what I should do, I remembered a magazine article I'd read that week about helping children become "can do kids."

Raising Can Do Kids

"Andrew," I said, "Mommy has decided to give you a new name. From this moment forward you are going to be my '*can do kid*.' In fact, we are going to have a new rule. You are no longer allowed to say, 'I can't,' because, Andrew, there are so many things you *can do*. Mommy is going to help you, and I will even do them with you."

It was time for dinner, so I told Andrew we were going to set the table together. I handed him the forks and showed him where each one went. I gave him one plate and cup at a time and watched him complete each setting. He was so proud of himself. Once he finished, Andrew looked at me and said, "Mommy, I *can* do it!"

What often holds our children back is a lack of confidence and courage. Just like Andrew, many kids measure their abilities based on how well they can do something compared to someone else. And there will always be a friend or sibling who can do it just a little better.

That day taught me an important lesson: my children need me to believe in them and to demonstrate it through my words and actions. Looking back, I could see the steps I took:

- I drew Andrew's attention away from something he couldn't do and helped him focus on something he *could* do.
- I showed him how to do it, and then I did it with him.
- Once he gained his confidence, I stepped back and watched as he completed his assignment with success.
- We celebrated and talked about how good it felt to do new things.

That night I introduced Andrew with his new name at the dinner table, and we all started calling Andrew our "can do kid." Several weeks later, Joshua offered to help Andrew feed our dogs. Much to all of our surprise, Andrew said, "Thanks, but I don't need any help. I'm a can do kid!"

Giving Our Children Courage

Andrew's "I can't" revealed some underlying fear and insecurity. It wasn't that he couldn't, it was that he didn't have the confidence to see if he could. He needed me to believe in him and give him the courage to take a chance and do something he did not know how to do.

Without fear, our children don't need courage. But with courage they can face their fear and prove to themselves it was worth the risk, even if they fail. Because the worst failure of all is knowing you never tried.

By believing in your kids, you can instill in them the courage they need to overcome the fears, insecurities, and doubts that hold them back. Through your encouraging words and your presence, you tell your children you believe in them and will be with them as they persevere and overcome the hard stuff.

> It wasn't that he couldn't, it was that he didn't have the confidence to see if he could.

Here are some simple ways to let your children know you believe in them:

- When you see something good, tell your child specifically what you noticed.
- Get on their level and look them in the eyes when you are talking to them.
- If you notice something they do wrong, don't mention it until you have told them at least three things they've done right.

Filling Them Up before They Need It

When she was three our daughter, Aster, was diagnosed with global developmental delays, a sensory processing disorder, and a speech disorder. From the time she was four, our sweet girl has had an extensive IEP (individual education plan). Two years ago, at age ten, Aster went through a series of evaluations at school that were part of an in-depth review of her academics, social skills, self-help skills, and intellectual abilities. When we met with her IEP team to review the test results, it became clear that Aster's scores were lower than we all hoped they'd be, and she needed more resources and supports. This meant she would be pulled out of her mainstream classroom more than 40 percent of her school day. J.J. and I walked out of the meeting with heavy hearts and no idea what our daughter's future would look like.

I cried that afternoon thinking about how Aster's confidence could be impacted long term, and how her peers might treat her when her learning disabilities became more obvious. Although Aster didn't know we had a meeting with her school that morning or what her test results were, I wondered how aware she was of her disabilities and if they were affecting her mentally or emotionally. She had to work extra hard at everything, including friendships, and I knew she did not like that anyone thought she needed more help at school than other kids.

That afternoon, I decided not to wait until I knew Aster needed encouragement. Instead, I wanted to be proactive and fill her tank up before she even got close to empty. After snack time, I asked Aster to turn off the television and come to the kitchen because I had something important to tell her.

When she got over to me, I bent down to her eye level and made sure I had her full attention. I placed my hands gently on her shoulders and told her, "I want you to know something: Aster, *you are enough*, just as you are! You don't have to do anything more to be enough. I love you just the way you are!"

She looked at me with a big smile and hugged me tight. There were no words spoken, but her eyes were saying, *Really?*, like a child being told they were getting a puppy. It was a grin of gratitude and disbelief.

I think it is important to make extra-large deposits of encouragement in our kids' hearts before they ever need them. That afternoon, as I was talking to Jesus about my concerns and how hard it is to know what Aster needs, I sensed Him telling me not to wait until someone hurts her feelings or until signs of insecurities surface. Instead, I could make deposits of encouragement as part of a building effort instead of a rescue mission to repair damage.

> It is important to make extra-large deposits of encouragement in our kids' hearts before they ever need them.

Wouldn't it be amazing if we could pour so much encouragement into our kids that there would be no room for discouragement to get in? I know that's not entirely possible, but perhaps we could be so intentional about filling their hearts up that when insults come they are a lot less likely to believe them.

Lord, help me encourage my children and build them up (1 Thess. 5:11) through the power of affirmation and encouraging words. It's such an important responsibility, and I know the more I seek You and make time for You to pour encouragement into my heart, the more I will have to give. Remind me of the ways You helped Your children (like Moses, Gideon, Peter, and others) become can do kids by getting them to focus on the promise of Your presence with them and Your potential in them. Amen.

53

seven

Your Child Needs to Know Character Matters Most

Once upon a time there were three little pigs who grew up and moved out on their own. Each pig immediately decided to build a house so he could live happily ever after with his pretty piglet princess. Well, okay, that isn't exactly how the story goes, but it is how I always wanted it to go. Why couldn't the first two pigs have wised up and used better building materials?

When the big bad wolf came huffing and puffing, two of the three houses came tumbling down. But the third pig took his time and built with materials that would last, and his house stood firm. And every time their story is told, the same lesson is learned: *be careful what you build with.*

A Firm Foundation

Jesus tells a similar story in Luke 6:46–49. He describes the choices every builder makes. He says those who listen to what He says and live by His words are like builders who dig deep and lay a foundation on rock. He also warns that those who hear His words and don't live by them are building without any foundation.

The first option gives us a life and a legacy that will withstand the storms. The second option is like building on a foundation that will be washed away by the storms of life. Jesus tells us the same thing I wanted to tell those little pigs: be careful what you build with; it determines how your story ends.

In *Raising Great Kids*, Drs. Henry Cloud and John Townsend write,

> We are building something really important. And what we build with will absolutely influence what our kids decide to use to build their own lives. It's simple. We are constructing a life. We do so primarily by the choices we make . . . and the quality of choices we make will determine the quality of our character, our soul.[1]

They describe character "as the sum of our abilities to deal with life as God designed us" and explain that the reality of life requires certain things from us, such as the ability to "relate to other people in good ways, to do what we say we will do, to take ownership of our own mistakes, and to solve our own problems. Our success (or failure) in meeting these demands shows our level of character development."[2]

Strong Building Materials

We are all building something. Brick by brick, through the choices we make, we construct lives that reflect what we value. The decisions we make and the things we celebrate tell our children what matters most to us. You see, we are not only building *our* lives; we are also laying a foundation for our children to build on as well. By noting and nurturing our children's character, we give them building materials that will withstand the test of time.

One thing I love about character development is that it doesn't require a high IQ, academic giftedness, or athletic ability. Every child has a chance to succeed and make a difference. When we make character the focus of our parenting, our children's potential is unlimited.

A Life of Love

When character matters most, our thoughts are more focused on how we treat others. In Matthew 7:12, Jesus tells us, "In everything, treat others as you would want them to treat you, for this fulfills the law and the prophets" (NET). Character turns our children's attention outward, and ours too.

> When character matters most, it gives us all a reason to focus on others and find God's purpose in living and loving like Jesus.

When character matters most, it gives us all a reason to focus on those around us and find God's purpose in living and loving them like Jesus. Ephesians 5:1–2 tells us, "Imitate God, therefore, in everything you do, because you are his dear children. Live a life filled with love, following the example of Christ" (NLT). If our kids know that honesty, perseverance, acceptance, generosity, compassion, patience, loyalty, and kindness are core values, we'll teach them to live a life of love by being kind to their friends, family, and even strangers.

Getting Started

When we started using our Mining for Gold Character Chart, I explained to my kids the parallel between gold in the ground and gold in their hearts. Then I shared the list of golden attitudes and actions and explained how each character trait reflects Jesus's heart toward us, and in us, because we are created in His image.

I also explained the dirt: our not-so-golden actions and attitudes that bury all the good stuff. And eventually I found a creative way to deal with that dirt, which I will share more about later in this section.

To start off, we decided to focus on a new trait each week, which helped us shift our mindsets to making character matter most. On Saturday morning or Sunday afternoon we chose the character trait for the next week and read the simple definition I'd come up with for the trait, along with a Scripture that went with it. We would also make a list of ways to put that week's trait into action throughout the week.

For instance, the week we focused on patience, here is what our character trait card included:

Be **PATIENT**.
Wait without complaining.
"Be patient, bearing with one another in love" (Eph. 4:2).
• Ask for something and then wait without asking again.
• Be patient with yourself when you don't know how to do something.
• Don't interrupt. Wait for your turn to talk.
• Have each family member wait to buy something they really want.

That week, I looked for examples in the Bible to read to them about times when Jesus was patient. My main goal was for my kids to get to know Jesus by seeing how He lived and loved others and them. As the week went on, I also pointed out characters in a storybook or asked them about characters in their favorite TV shows who were being patient or impatient. At mealtime and bedtime, J.J. and I shared examples of how we were patient or needed to be patient during the day (at work and at home, with them or with each other).

I've found that the best way to develop character in our kids is by learning about each trait together and looking for simple ways to put God's love and kindness into action. Near the end of the book, I have included everything you need with twenty-four character traits to help you get started.

Look for Preexisting Gold

Discover your kids' strengths by looking for attributes that come naturally to them. This will give your new adventure a positive start.

- Is your child *compassionate*—caring about someone who got hurt?
- Is your child *accepting*—making friends with someone who looks different from them?
- Is your child *responsible*—taking out the trash or making the bed without being asked?
- Is your child *forgiving*—willing to overlook an offense?

Celebrate Progress

When you notice your children showing character in their actions or attitude, stop what you are doing and tell them right away. That way they will start to recognize what it looks like to be patient, to be accepting, to be content, to take initiative, and so on.

If you want a tangible way to celebrate your kids' progress, here is what I did. One afternoon I decided to create gold nuggets by balling up foil and spray painting these "nuggets" gold. When I saw my kids displaying a golden attitude or action, I gave them a gold nugget. I also got some small jars for them to keep their nuggets in and set up a simple system to redeem them.

More details, simple steps to create a gold nugget system for younger kids to redeem special treats, and family activities can be found at reneeswope.com/a-confident-mom/gold-nuggets.

Making It Fun

Although I was the one who initiated the idea of mining for gold, J.J. loved the idea and was on board from day one. He is a kid at heart, so he decided to add some fun by making up games to help teach the kids the traits we were learning.

The week we focused on encouragement, he put M&Ms in a cup at one end of the room and had Joshua stand at the other side of the room. Then he tied a blanket around Joshua's waist and told him to pull against the resistance to get to the M&Ms while Dad held the ends of the blanket.

While Joshua pulled, J.J. shouted discouraging comments like "You might as well give up. You'll never get to the other side. It's not worth it to work so hard."

Then I coached Andrew on how to cheer his big brother on with encouraging statements like "You can do it. Don't give up!"

Finally, J.J. loosened the pull of the blanket and allowed Joshua to get to the cup. While they ate M&Ms together, J.J. talked with Joshua and Andrew about the rewards of not giving up, even when things are hard, and about the power of encouragement in helping someone else persevere.

Having fun and putting actions to the Bible verses and character traits we were studying helped our kids see that following God is an adventure, and that God's Word is applicable and helpful for our everyday life.

Just like starting anything new, it will take time and reminders to help you focus on noticing and nurturing character in your kids. It is helpful to put sticky notes on the refrigerator, on the mirror, and in the car with reminders to notice the gold and not the dirt. No matter what, have fun and watch God shape your children's hearts and your own to be more like His each day!

Lord, I want to give my children a solid foundation to build their lives on by making sure they know their character matters most. Help me set aside time to assess the materials we are using to lay our foundation and come up with a simple and fun plan to learn and live character with my kids. I want us to live a life of love, imitating You in everything we do as we discover and develop the gold of Your image in us. Amen.

eight

Your Child Needs to Know the Bible Is More Than a Story

All throughout Scripture, God shows us how to live and how to love. And He gives detailed instructions to parents about sharing His Word and His ways with our kids. In Deuteronomy 6, He tells us,

> Love the LORD your God with all your heart and with all your soul and with all your strength. These commandments that I give you today are to be on your hearts. Impress them on your children. Talk about them when you sit at home and when you walk along the road, when you lie down and when you get up. Tie them as symbols on your hands and bind them on your foreheads. Write them on the doorframes of your houses and on your gates. (vv. 5–9)

It's clear that God doesn't want the Bible to be just a book or a story we read to our children, or with them, during family devotions or bedtime routines. He wants His Word to be alive and active in our homes and part of our everyday lives and conversations.

Talking about God's Word with our children all day, every day, can feel like an overwhelming and insurmountable task. We already have so many things to think about, so many tasks to complete, and then there are the children who have zero interest. But God doesn't want it to feel impossible or overwhelming. In fact, I think He wants it to be a simple, easy overflow of our relationship with Him into our relationship with our children.

Weaving God's Word into Everyday Life

I started by looking for creative ways to talk about God when we were at the dinner table, when I sat on the edge of our children's beds or on the couch with them after school, or when we took a walk around our neighborhood. It doesn't need to be complicated, profound, or power-packed. God just wants us to weave His Word into our daily lives and invite His perspective into our conversations.

We can talk about God while we are running errands or sitting in the carpool line. We can share with our kids something we noticed in our devotional, a Scripture we are focusing on that day, or a promise we are holding on to through a struggle we are facing. We can share a story we read in our Bible.

> God wants His Word to be alive and active in our homes and part of our everyday lives and conversations.

We can talk about God's perspective when our children share about something going on in their day or something going on in our family.

Whether you are reading Bible stories with your children or on your own, start looking for God's character in the ways He interacted with and led His people in the Old Testament and in the ways Jesus related to His disciples, curious seekers, and sinners in the New Testament.

Take time to read the Bible with your children in a version that is best suited for their ages. One of my favorites is the *Jesus*

Storybook Bible. Start out by reading about Jesus's life and ask your kids what traits are being reflected in the stories. All throughout the Gospels, you will see how Jesus reflects the character traits in my list of golden attitudes and actions.

We would often weave the Bible verses that correspond with each character trait into a family devotion. Sometimes we'd play a guessing game by reading a verse and then having the kids guess what trait was being described. Or someone would name a trait and everybody else would have to come up with the verse that goes with it or name a Bible character and story where the character trait is displayed. Whoever wins gets to decide what's for dessert!

When our kids were little, we would make up songs with the words of the Scripture verses to help them learn them. As they got older, we encouraged them to write the verses on index cards and gave them incentives for memorizing them.

Grow on the Go

Time in the car is such a great time to talk with our children about ways we can put God's love into action as we run errands or interact with each other. When we weave God's Word into our everyday lives, it helps our kids see that following God and developing a heart like His is not about rules and regulations. It's about living an adventure with Him that's built on a relationship. We are loved by Him, and we show our love for Him and others through attitudes and actions that reflect His heart.

Although I love the convenience of returning calls on my speakerphone while I'm driving, having my kids' attention in the car has been

> I try to remind myself I will always have texts and calls to return, but I won't always have times like these younger years, with a captive audience in the back seat.

an opportunity I knew I wouldn't always have. I'm not saying I never return calls when Aster is in the car with me, but when I get into a pattern of doing that 90 percent of the time, I try to remind myself I will always have texts and calls to return, but I won't always have times like these younger years, with a captive audience in the back seat.

Be Doers of God's Word

One month, when we were focused on sharing, we memorized Hebrews 13:16, "Do not forget to do good and to share with others," and decided to share our food by taking a meal to friends who had recently moved. I loved knowing that my kids were learning how to be doers of God's Word and not just hearers, which is what God wants (James 1:22).

The week we focused on contentment, we learned Hebrews 13:5, "Keep your lives free from the love of money and be content with what you have." That week we decided not to buy anything new, and we started a "Gratitude Journal."

It's so important for our children to see that Scripture isn't a book of rules and regulations; it's more like a road map—for life. Putting Scripture into action together helps them, and us, see that. It's a great way to get your children to think about how they can apply what the Bible says to their actions, their attitude, their friendships, and more. Then, at dinner, in the car, or at bedtime, let your collective ideas and actions become conversation starters as you talk with your kids about how you are weaving God's Word and His ways into your everyday lives.

More Than a Story

"I'm writing a book at school," Joshua shouted from the back of our minivan.

"That's great. What's it about?" I asked.

"It's about a boy named Jaylan who goes to the beach with his family and gets stung by a stingray. The next day he's afraid to go in the water. But that night he reads his Bible and remembers the story about David. He prays and asks God to give him courage to go swimming again. And the next day when his parents want to go in the ocean, he goes and they are really surprised."

"That's awesome, Josh!" I turned around and gave him a big smile. And as I did, he said, "And tomorrow I am going to write the next chapter where he's being bullied at school, and he's going to read about Zacchaeus and learn about forgiveness."

J.J. and I looked at each other and grinned. It had been four years since God had gotten hold of my heart and changed my perspective on parenting. Four years since we'd started trying to make God and the Bible a natural part of our everyday lives. Four years of looking for ways to live what Scripture said in our relationships with each other and those around us.

Joshua was taking the main character in his book through struggles and fears he had faced himself the past year. A jellyfish sting that summer. Fears of going in the ocean again. A bully at school. Learning to forgive. He was walking a storybook character who represented himself through the process of looking to God's Word for answers to his problems and courage to face his fears.

Joshua telling us about his book was God's kindness to two imperfect parents. We had made so many mistakes along the way over those four years. But that's the thing about God. He takes the little we have to offer and makes it enough. And He used that moment in the minivan to encourage us to keep going and to show us that what we were doing was making a difference, even if we couldn't always see it.

That day we got a glimpse of possibility. Maybe our child was starting to understand the Bible as more than a story or rules to follow. It is a map written by his Maker to light the way as God directs his heart and his path through life!

Lord, help our family to follow Your example, as dearly loved children, and walk in the way of love, just as Christ loved us and gave Himself up for us as a fragrant offering and sacrifice to God. I want to intentionally find ways to make Your Word a part of our family's everyday life, and I know it all starts with my heart and my relationship with You. Please give me a sense of purpose as I invest time in shaping my kids' hearts and not just their habits. As we focus on Your Word and look for ways to live it out, I know You will take our hearts and make them more like Yours. Holy Spirit, I depend on You to guide me as I commit myself wholeheartedly to the truths You are teaching me today. Amen.

nine

Your Child Needs to Know They're Worth Listening To

I was upstairs getting ready for bed one night when I heard J.J. calling Chelsea, our thirteen-year-old dachshund, in a really sweet voice to come get her treat. I knew it was his way of luring her to the back door and then to her doggie bed in the laundry room.

Daisy, our beagle, was already in the backyard doing her business, anticipating the reward of a doggy biscuit if she obediently came back inside and went to her bed.

J.J. eventually gave up and went looking for Chelsea, who was sound asleep in her favorite chair in our den, unwilling to budge. When J.J. and the boys came upstairs, I asked them if they thought Chelsea had "selective hearing" skills because she didn't want to go to bed or if she was going deaf. I had a feeling it was the latter. We joked about how Chelsea used to hear everything. Whether it was the ice maker in our kitchen or the wind blowing the leaves outside, she heard it and barked at it.

But a few minutes later, when Josh had left the room, Andrew, who was nine at the time, came to me with a concerned look in his eyes and said, "Mom, I hope when you get old you don't go deaf like Chelsea."

I laughed and told him that when I get as old as Chelsea, it might be good if I can't hear everything because she gets a lot more sleep than I do. Plus, I explained, she doesn't hear us laughing about her, and I'll probably be better off not hearing jokes about me either.

My lighthearted response didn't wipe the concern off his brow, so I asked why he was afraid I wouldn't be able to hear him.

He answered without hesitation, "Well, sometimes you don't hear me now. Like when you're on the computer and I ask you a question, sometimes you don't hear me."

Ouch. I was not expecting to find out my child thought I couldn't hear him. His answer almost plunged me into a "bad mom" moment with flashbacks of all the times I'd heard him but didn't listen because I was deeply distracted.

What They Have to Say Matters

Instead of defining that moment with shame and guilt, I pulled Andrew close and told him I was sorry for not listening sometimes. Since I didn't want him to fear that old age might make it worse, I explained how me being on the computer was like him watching a good movie or playing video games, when his brain is so involved that it's almost like he's in another world and can't hear me calling him for dinner. He nodded with a smile, and I could see his concern fade.

My example helped him understand, but I didn't want it to become

> Instead of defining that moment with shame and guilt, I pulled Andrew close and told him I was sorry for not listening sometimes.

67

an excuse to make me feel better. So, I made him a promise that I hoped I could keep.

"Andrew," I said, "what you have to say matters to me. I'm going to try really hard when you come to me to stop what I am doing, look away from my computer, and listen to what you're saying. You're more important than anything I do on the computer. Please forgive me for the times I don't listen."

Psalm 17:6 reminds me of our human longing to be heard:

> I am praying to you because I know you will answer,
> O God.
> Bend down and listen as I pray. (NLT)

In the same way we go to God because we want Him to listen and answer us, our children come to us because they want to be listened to and heard. Being heard gives them a sense of connectedness, which is something every child needs.

The Gift of Listening

That night God showed me a valuable gift He offers me and wants me to give my children: the gift of listening. I give it each time I simply stop what I'm doing and give my full attention to them when they want to talk to me.

The best listening advice I've heard is found in the Bible: "Everyone should be quick to listen, [and] slow to speak" (James 1:19). Basically, keep our mouths closed and our ears open. But I think God would take it a step further and encourage us to listen with our whole heart by leaning in and really hearing what our kids are saying instead of thinking about what we want to say next.

There are so many distractions around me that challenge my listening skills, along with the gazillion thoughts inside my head that come with ADHD. Listening well is something I've really had to work at over the years. But with practice, I have gotten so much better.

Here are a few simple ways to listen well so your children know they are worth listening to.

Give Your Undivided Attention

- Set aside your agenda and listen to them.
- Silence your cell phone.
- Make and keep eye contact.
- Lean in and make sure nonverbal cues communicate that you are paying attention.
- Pray as you listen. Ask God to give you wisdom and discernment to process your child's spoken and unspoken thoughts and concerns.

Put Yourself in Their Shoes

- Empathize with their feelings and emotions.
- Let the interaction be about them, not you.
- Don't be afraid to laugh, cry, celebrate, or be still with them.

Ask Good Questions

- Without interrupting, ask open-ended questions to clarify your understanding: "So, what I hear you saying is . . . ?" Open-ended questions tell them you want to make sure you hear and understand what they are saying.

Convey Unconditional Love

- It's okay if they fall short of your expectations; lean in and listen with appreciation for one of God's unique children.
- Listening well doesn't mean you are condoning bad behavior or agreeing with how they handled a situation; it means

you respect them and simply want to give them the gift of listening through your time and attention.

In our culture of constant contact through texts, social media, cell phones, apps, and multiple devices, our attention is divided, and our focus is so often shifted away from those who are in the room with us. Our children need to know they are worth more than the screens in our hands and the competing thoughts in our heads. We don't need to let them dominate our attention all the time, but when we listen with our whole heart on a regular basis, we give our children a deep sense of value that will build over time and a connectedness with their hearts that will last long into their adult years.

> Our children need to know they are worth more than the screens in our hands and the competing thoughts in our heads.

Lord, I'm so grateful for the incredible fact that You listen to me. Please help me become a better listener and make sure my children know they are worth listening to. I confess sometimes I hear with one ear while the other is turned toward something else. I want to give the gift of listening to my kids and listening well, so they know I value them and what they have to say. Help me be aware of when I'm not listening and be willing to turn my attention to them so I can become a good listener like You. Amen.

ten

Your Child Needs to Feel Your Acceptance and Approval

When Joshua was little, he was extremely shy and did not like big social settings, which included fall festivals, Christmas parties, family reunions, Easter egg hunts, and neighborhood parades. In my mind, he didn't like all the fun stuff.

When he was three years old, I dressed him up in a cute Hershey's Kiss costume to wear to our church's indoor fall festival. I envisioned taking lots of photos of him and his best buddy smiling and posing in front of the bales of hay. But instead, as soon as we walked through the gymnasium doors, Joshua clung to my leg like a koala bear. He refused to go play with the other kids and would barely say hi to his best friend.

I tried everything to get him to stop hiding behind my knees, but nothing worked. I chatted with other parents as I watched their kids jumping in the bounce house, chasing each other, comparing costumes, playing games, and posing for photos. I was sad because I wanted Joshua to have fun, and I felt bad when a few mom friends tried unsuccessfully to talk him into playing with their kids. I also got the impression some thought I should push him a little harder to socialize. And, on top of all that, I wanted to walk around and see all the decorations and festivities without a little boy holding on to my leg for dear life.

It kills me to admit this now, but, in situations like that one, I wished my little boy was like other kids: talkative, outgoing, and playful with his peers. But once I understood my child and accepted him, I was able to get to know the depths of who God uniquely created Joshua to be. And I wouldn't want to change a thing about him. How I wish I could go back and tell him that then!

If I knew then what I know now, I would still have gone to the festival, but I would have adjusted my expectations. And when Joshua grabbed my leg, instead of trying to pry him off, I would have bent down and looked him in the eye and said, "Let's walk around together."

But that is not where I was in my motherhood journey. I had lots of growing and learning to do. The most important thing I've learned as a mom over the past twenty-six years is that it's never too late to say things you wish you'd said or do things you wish you'd done.

Uniquely Designed

God uniquely designed our children with preferences and individual personalities. In Psalm 139, King David describes the intricacy of God's creativity and the intimacy of His knowing us from head to toe:

> You created my inmost being;
> you knit me together in my mother's womb.

I praise you because I am fearfully and wonderfully made;
　　your works are wonderful,
　　I know that full well.
My frame was not hidden from you
　　when I was made in the secret place,
　　when I was woven together in the depths of the earth.
Your eyes saw my unformed body;
　　all the days ordained for me were written in your book
　　before one of them came to be. (vv. 13–16)

Just like us, our children also have a God-given longing to know their parents delight in their quirks and qualms as well as their ideas and interests. There is no one whose approval and acceptance matters more to our children than ours.

Accepting our children is not always easy, especially if they are not what we expected or hoped for when we envisioned being a parent. It's challenging when our children don't have the same interests or personality as we do, or when our hopes and expectations don't fit into the way God created them. That is when we have to open our hands and let go of what we wanted, so we can get to know and enjoy the child God gave us.

Our daughter has special needs that greatly impact her desire and ability to communicate and connect. I've grieved the loss of what I hoped and dreamed of doing with my little girl, and what I thought our relationship would look like down the road. Is there an expectation or hope that you may need to surrender to make room for acceptance and for taking an interest in who your child is, instead of being disappointed in who they aren't? It's okay to feel sad or let down, and it's healthy to name the hopes you had and grieve the loss of them.

Our children will probably experience ridicule and rejection from others at some point, but our homes should be where our kids experience the strongest sense of approval and acceptance they can find in the world.

You Are Special

You Are Special by Max Lucado is the story of a small village filled with wooden people called Wemmicks.[1] Each day the little Wemmicks go around putting stars and dot stickers on each other, based on how they look and what they can or can't do. Punchinello, the main character of the story, is made of wood that is chipped with paint that is peeling, which means he is also covered with gray dots from head to toe.

One day Punchinello meets a girl who doesn't have any stars or dots. Curious, he asks her why, and she explains it's because she visits Eli, the woodcarver, in his woodshop each day. Although he doubts Eli would want to see him, Punchinello musters up the courage to visit the woodcarver.

During his visit with Eli, Punchinello discovers that the one who made him thinks he's special. Eli tells Punchinello he doesn't care what others think about him, and he shouldn't either. After their visit, Punchinello turns to leave, and Eli tells him, "You are special because I made you, and I don't make mistakes." Punchinello doesn't understand, but in his heart he starts to believe Eli means it, and when he does a gray dot falls to the ground.

It's Hard to Give What We Don't Have

Our children need to know God thinks they are special—and we do too! But it is hard to give our children acceptance and approval if we don't offer ourselves the same.

Sincere and lasting acceptance for your children and for yourself will come from an overflow of finding your true worth from the One who created you. Just like Eli the woodcarver, God invites you to come to Him every day and let Him remind you of how He sees you and how much He cares about you. He wants to tell you every single day, "You are special because I made you, and I don't make mistakes!"

The more we receive God's acceptance and believe His affirmation, the more we will have to give away.

Avoiding Criticism and Comparison

The opposite of acceptance and approval are criticism and comparison. Punchinello had been controlled by the enemy of comparison and crippled by the criticism of others. One of my concerns for my kids is that they would be marked by the culture we live in, which can feel like that little town of wooden people who go around sticking stars and dots on each other.

Home needs to be a place where our children can find refuge and encouragement to combat the messages of our culture, which are filled with criticism and comparison. With and without words, our kids are told every day that their worth is based on what they have, how much they are liked, and how well they are doing compared to others. And we've got to make sure that is not also happening in our homes. Comparison and criticism only pile on the dirt that will bury us and them.

Our children are much more likely to do what we do and not what we say, which means if they see us depending on our identity in Christ and seeking God's value of us for our worth, they are more likely to do the same. If they hear us constantly criticizing our flaws, they will constantly be thinking about theirs.

> God wants us to look for and celebrate our children's natural tendencies and unique traits. When we do, we will discover a child who makes the world a better place because they are in it!

What we look for is what we will find. God wants us to look for and celebrate our children's natural tendencies and unique traits. When we do, we will discover a child who makes the world a better place because they are in it!

Lord, thank You for the children You have given me to love! I confess I have had expectations that sometimes blind me from seeing the unique way You have created them. And I want to not only accept my child but really enjoy my child. I pray You would fill my heart and my mouth with words of affirmation, approval, and acceptance to speak over them. Teach me the language of approval and affirmation as I hear You speak it over me. Help me to slow down and see my children through Your eyes and cherish the unique way You made them and the interests You've given them. Amen.

eleven

Your Child Needs to Feel Known and Understood

I once heard my friend Gary describe the difference in how God creates and how people create: "When we look at God's creation, we see uneven edges and variations in color with twists and turns in many shapes. But when we look at manmade creations—for instance, buildings—they all line up and are squared off, so everything fits together nicely."

Gary pointed out how God's creation is a lot more *creative*. He said it's like comparing people and potatoes to hot dogs. God made people and potatoes, and you can't find any two people or potatoes exactly alike. But hot dogs are all the same shape and size. They all fit in a bun, and they're boring.

It was such a good reminder. As a mom, I need to remember my kids are not like hot dogs. They are like potatoes, creatively designed by God to be different. But don't we sometimes wish they were like hot dogs that fit into nice, neat little packages so they would be easier to figure out and keep straight?

A Personality Potato Bar

I love a good potato bar with all the toppings: cheddar cheese, sour cream, scallions, chili, butter, bacon bits, and chives. Most of the time, though, I stick to my preferences and only add butter, cheese, and bacon bits to my potato. I'm usually the first one to the table, so I watch as everyone else in our family comes through the line. Even though we all have the same options to choose from, none of our potatoes ever look alike.

When God created our children, he gave them individual personalities that are a unique combination of toppings that include their desires, emotional needs, strengths, and challenges. Understanding our children's personalities, and affirming their uniqueness, is one of the greatest gifts we can give them.

> Understanding our children's personalities, and affirming their uniqueness, is one of the greatest gifts we can give them.

My favorite book for learning about our children's personalities is *Personality Plus for Parents* by Florence Littauer. Here is a quick overview of the personality types from Littauer's work, which I highly recommend.[1]

Phlegmatic Personality

A phlegmatic's number one *goal* in life is to have peace. Phlegmatic children are low-key and easygoing. They have a good sense of humor and don't get upset easily. They bring balance to their relationships and usually have few enemies because they are so likable.

- Their *motto* is: Let's do it the easy way.
- Their *emotional needs* include peace and quiet, down time, and a feeling of worth.

- Their *strengths* include the tendency to be calm and peaceful. They are the peacemakers who are steady, consistent, and kind, and they are great listeners too.
- Their *challenges* include being hard to motivate, resistant to exertion, and conflict avoidant. They can also be stubborn and tend to procrastinate.

Choleric Personality

A choleric's number one *goal* in life is control. Choleric children are dependable, hard workers, and natural born leaders. They like to have a sense of control and can be counted on to get things done. They also have strong opinions and aren't shy about sharing them.

- Their *motto* is: Just do it.
- Their *emotional need*s are control, appreciation, loyalty, and getting credit.
- Their *strengths* include being organized, task-oriented, and competent. They are gifted at seeing a situation, thinking through things, and coming to a right conclusion.
- Their *challenges* include being overly determined, stubborn, and strong-willed. They want to be in control and do things their way, which sometimes comes across as bossy, rude, and inconsiderate.

Sanguine Personality

A sanguine's number one *goal* in life is to have fun. Sanguine children are energetic, loving, adventurous, and fun. They enjoy quality time with friends and family, enjoy being the center of attention, and are often very entertaining.

- Their *motto* is: Let's do it the fun way.
- Their *emotional needs* include attention, affection, and a sense of approval.

79

- Their *strengths* include their ability to make friends quickly, a great sense of humor, and storytelling abilities. They can charm their way into all kinds of situations and out of all kinds of trouble.
- Their *challenges* include attention-seeking, which can overshadow others. They tend to back out of commitments if they aren't fun, and they are sensitive to criticism and take it extremely personally.

Melancholy Personality

A melancholy's number one *goal* is perfection. Melancholy children are thoughtful and sensitive. They work well alone and strive for perfection. They are also careful, organized, and have great attention for details.

- Their *motto* is: Let's do it the right way.
- Their *emotional needs* include sensitivity, space, solitude, and quiet.
- Their *strengths* include being able to work well alone and having an artistic sensibility along with the ability to be analytical. They love schedules, accuracy, and rules to follow.
- Their *challenges* include being shy, clingy, perfectionistic, afraid to fail, sensitive to criticism, and seeing problems instead of solutions. They can also be moody.

Do you recognize your child or children in any of these personality descriptions? Do you see why they may act the way they do or have preferences that are different from yours? Learning the motivation, strengths, challenges, and emotional needs of these four personality types was a game-changer for me! Recognizing I am sanguine and Joshua is melancholy, for example, enabled me to see why our needs, motivations, and strengths were so different.

Florence Littauer says,

> If you listen, you will understand what makes your children tick. Ask them how they feel about each other, about you, and about their teacher; then listen. Do they talk about fun? Tell you what to do? Aim for perfection? Or take it easy? They will tell you if you take time to listen, and then you can meet their emotional needs, saving them from a lifetime of searching for what they never got as a child.[2]

Seeing and Valuing Their Differences

A few years after the fall festival incident, Joshua's first grade teacher called me one day and told me she was really worried about him. When I asked why, she told me it was because he never did anything wrong. That sounds like the call every parent wants, right? But she was concerned he might get an ulcer or never learn to enjoy school.

I told her he was pretty compliant at home too, except when he turned three years old and we had a war going on between us for a few weeks. And then, of course, when he turned into a teenager. Also, as an adult he has since confessed he was compliant in front of us but a little bit sneaky behind our backs, especially when his younger brother came along.

Anyway, about first grade. I assured his teacher we didn't expect perfect behavior from Joshua. We decided she would watch for Joshua to do something in class that would warrant his getting a small markdown. That way he would see it wasn't a big ordeal if he did something wrong.

A few days later, Joshua came home from school with his head down. Staring at the floor, he confessed he had gotten "his ticket pulled," which meant his teacher gave him a warning for not listening. He was shocked when I lifted his chin, looked in his eyes, and said with a smile, "That's okay! Just try to listen better tomorrow."

Of course, I wanted him to respect authority, but as he was a child who swung his pendulum toward perfection, I wanted him to see it was okay to make a mistake.

Andrew was a different story. He leaned toward sanguine and choleric tendencies and had absolutely no fear of consequences. His teacher did not call to tell me she was concerned because he never did anything wrong. She called to tell me Andrew lost his recess time because he had turned building blocks into imaginary guns and wouldn't obey when she told him to stop hiding under the table pretending to be a cowboy shooting bad guys.

I'm still trying to figure out what Aster's personality is, because she seems to be an even mix of all four types. What about your kids? Are you starting to recognize them in the personality type descriptions? Does it help to know their needs, tendencies, strengths, and challenges?

The more I learned about my kids' personalities, the more I was able to notice and point out their strengths to them too. I encourage you to be intentional about telling your kids how they are uniquely designed by God, for a purpose, created in Christ Jesus to do the good things He planned for each of us long ago (Eph. 2:10).

> Let's remember our kids are in process, becoming all that God created them to be, just like us when we were growing up—and just like us today.

The environment of our home shapes our children's perspective of themselves, of God, and of life. Let's create a home where our potatoes can grow in the soil of acceptance and approval. A home where they know they are loved for who they are and liked for how they are. A home where our kids, whether young or old, don't feel pressured to be the product of their parents' desires or efforts. A home where everyone's needs and preferences are honored, and where each person is encouraged to discover and develop their unique interests, abilities, strengths, and challenges.

And let's remember our kids are in process, becoming all that God created them to be, just like us when we were growing up—and just like us today.

Lord, help me to see my children's strengths and celebrate who they are as You designed them to be. I want to create a culture in our home where each of my children can thrive in their unique wiring that was handcrafted by You. Give me an overwhelming sense of Your love for my kids, even when they are hard to love or when I don't understand or relate to their needs and preferences. When they are living from the challenging parts of their personalities, remind me they are in process and this is a season, not a situation we will be in forever. Amen.

twelve

Your Child Needs to Feel Loved and Pursued

Andrew held a bag of valentines for his classmates on his lap, unfazed by the fact that his treats were not embellished with cartoon characters, hearts, or any indication of Valentine's Day. But I couldn't stop thinking about it.

The night before, Andrew reminded me that he was supposed to take valentines for his classmates the next day, and I had none. What kind of mom forgets Valentine's Day treats for her third grader? After we got the boys to bed, I ran to Target and frantically searched the Valentine's Day aisle, where I quickly discovered all the other moms had come early, and there were no more valentines or treats to be found. So I took the walk of shame down the regular candy aisle, where I found a plain bag of mini KitKat bars and decided to write "From Andrew" in Sharpie on the back of each treat.

This Is Love

As we sat together waiting in the morning carpool drop-off line, I wondered if I could make it up to him that afternoon by buying him something, but I wasn't sure what he would want. Before he got out of the car, I asked, "Andrew, what makes you feel loved?"

Andrew thought for a minute and said, "THIS."

"This?" I asked.

"Yeah. This. You being with me. You driving me to school and talking to me about my day. You telling me you'll be there when I get home. That makes me feel loved. Thanks, Mom. I love you, bye!" And he hopped out of the car.

This is love? You mean, I didn't have to work myself into a tizzy shopping for a toy to convince my child I wouldn't forget him even though I forget things that are important to him?

This is love? Even though I was grouchy the day before, so much so that Andrew asked if I was mad about something—more than once?

Yes, for Andrew, *my presence was love.* My being there that morning and promising to be there when he got home that afternoon. That is what made him feel loved more than anything else, but I didn't know it until he told me. And that is the day I realized that Andrew receives love through our being together.

Speaking Their Love Language

Like so many others, our family has been helped by the work of Dr. Gary Chapman, author of a wonderful series of books that use his concept of five love languages to explain how each of us predominantly expresses and understands love in one of five different ways.[1] Dr. Chapman's five love languages are quality time, acts of service, physical touch, gifts, and words of affirmation.

Of course, our kids need us to pursue their hearts and express our love for them in all five languages. But as they get older, it becomes more important for us to intentionally show our love in the way that makes them feel most loved.

Here are some simple ways we've expressed love to our kids using Dr. Chapman's love languages as a guide.

Quality Time

Spending quality time with our kids was something we tried and still try to do on a regular basis. Sometimes we would ride bikes, explore part of our city, watch a movie, or play a video game they love. We made sure to show up for important events in their lives. And we scheduled dates with them with the intention of getting to know them a little better each time. We also used that time to show them things we liked to do or places we liked to go.

From elementary school through high school, Andrew craved love through quality time together. When he got home from school, he wanted me to be available to talk to him. I didn't always succeed, but I tried my best to be at a good stopping place before he walked through the door. I also silenced my cell phone so we could talk and I could listen without interruptions and distractions.

Acts of Service

When our kids were younger, I would ask if they wanted help picking up their toys, or I'd offer to hang up their backpack or coat. As they got older and I was trying to teach them to be responsible, I was concerned that doing things to serve them would defeat that purpose. But I discovered my "you need to be responsible" life lessons weren't ruined if I occasionally did an act of service to help lighten their load. And I tried to let them know I did it because I loved them.

Some acts of service included me laying out an outfit for them the night before a big test, making their favorite breakfast, or bringing them a hot lunch at school. Sometimes I would grab their jacket out of the car when we got home and say, "I'll hang it up for you," instead of just doing it like it was my job.

Physical Touch

One of Andrew's and Aster's primary love languages is physical touch. It is also one of my primary love languages, so I naturally express my love with hugs, kisses, snuggles, soft pats on the back, and reading books while sitting close or with an arm around their shoulder. When our kids were younger, I would often cuddle up close with them on Saturday morning or wake them up with a kiss on their cheek if they slept in late.

As Joshua got older, I noticed physical touch wasn't one of his primary love languages, so I gave him more space. But because research shows that physical touch is a human need, no matter what, I try to stop what I am doing and greet my kids with a hug when they come home or when they leave, when I go out of town or when I get back, and before they go to bed at night—even with our sons and their wives when they spend the night at our house.

Gifts

Every child loves getting new stuff! So how do we know if it's their love language? And how do we show love through gifts without going broke? Will we spoil our child if we give them gifts on special occasions and not-so-special occasions?

A gift doesn't have to be expensive. It just needs to be a tangible object that says, *I thought about you, so I bought (or made) something to let you know it.* Joshua responded mostly to gifts growing up, so every once in a while I would surprise him with orange Tic Tacs from the grocery store or a book from the bookstore, and his sweet smile always told me he felt thought of and loved.

Recently, I noticed that whenever I surprise Aster with a small toy she wasn't expecting, she responds with a huge grin and a big hug, which isn't a typical response from her. She also makes me gifts or artwork to show her love, which tells me her primary love language is probably gifts.

Words of Affirmation

For a child who feels loved through words of affirmation, it's important to be specific, such as, "I like how you used different shades of gray in your drawing, and the shadowing you did here in this corner. You're a great artist!" They need extra encouragement and love when we notice the efforts and affirm their progress.

Another way we can love our kids with words of affirmation is through written notes and texts. We can also make digital messages, such as a short video with meaningful encouragement. When Andrew went off to college, he told me one of the things he was going to miss was J.J.'s encouraging sticky notes.

DR. CHAPMAN POINTS OUT that our children "absolutely need us to express love for them in all five love languages: touch, gifts, words of affirmation, deeds of service and quality time. And until they are around nine years old, determining their love language is challenging because they aren't able to verbalize what makes them feel most loved."[2] But there are little hints we can look for when our kids are five to eight years old:

- Ask your child to draw a picture of some ways a mommy can love her child.
- While you're reading a book or watching a video, ask, "How do you know if that mommy or daddy loves their little boy?"
- Pay attention to their drawings and answers for clues.

My children's primary love languages became more obvious around age ten. And as they got older, our boys and their wives completed a love language assessment, which helped them confirm their preferences and made it easier for all of us.

What matters most is that our children feel pursued and loved unconditionally, not because we told them on their last birthday but because we tell them and show them all the time, in more ways than one!

> What matters most is that our children feel pursued and loved unconditionally.

Lord, I pray You would help me notice and become more aware of the unique way each of my children perceives and receives love. I need Your help paying attention to how they show love with their actions and receive love through their reactions to my words of encouragement, touch, gifts, or quality time, or when I help them with something. Show me creative and easy ways to be more intentional about loving them in a language that speaks to their unique heart. Amen.

thirteen

Your Child Needs Connection and Belonging

I caught myself checking Instagram soon after I woke up. Twenty minutes later, I went downstairs, made breakfast, scrolled through Instagram again, and then hopped on Facebook.

I put down my phone, feeling like I needed to actually get something done, and decided to read my Bible and a devotional. When I was finished, I took a shower and got ready, pulled out my MacBook, and sat down at my desk to check email. Once my inbox was manageable, I hopped over to Instagram and Facebook—*again*.

It sounds crazy as I type it all out. And that day, when I caught myself checking social media a few times within a couple of hours, I wondered why I was doing it incessantly. Deep inside, I knew my constant checking was about more than keeping up with emails and social media updates.

My heart was craving something more. Finally, I paused to ask myself, *Why do I keep checking online?* I sat there for a moment, waiting for my heart to respond, and these words rose up in my thoughts: *You keep coming back because your heart longs for connection.*

Love the One You're With

I was trying to fill my need for real-life relationships with a screen and alphabet keys. But my heart craved something no amount of digital interactions could fill. And the same is true for our children. As much as they love their screens, they need real-life connection and a sense of belonging that is built through time together. Even with their own distractions, our children need our presence and our attention.

There were times when our boys were growing up that we would be together as a family, but my mind would be somewhere else getting something done! One Saturday night we were playing a board game and I was so proud of myself for leaving my phone in the kitchen and being fully present with them. Until I got distracted.

> As much as they love their screens, they need real-life connection and a sense of belonging that is built through time together.

Although my body was still in the living room, my mind had drifted off somewhere else, returning calls and texts in my head, making a grocery list, and thinking about all I could be getting done. I glanced at the clock across the room to see how many hours there were before the boys' bedtime, when I could get some work done. As I looked back at the game, Andrew's head was turned and all I could see was the silhouette of his face.

He looks so much older, I thought. It wouldn't be long before he started counting the hours until *I* went to bed so he could text friends and stay up late playing video games.

Lord, help me cherish and enjoy the gift of being with the ones I love while they're still with me, I prayed silently.

Together

Jesus knew His time on earth was limited, but He never seemed hurried or distracted. And I don't ever sense He saw people's desire for His time as an interruption, but rather He welcomed it as an invitation. He valued being with people over being productive.

Unlike Jesus, I tend to be a type-A, get-it-done kind of girl. *Being* instead of *doing* has always been hard for me. But I also know God wired me this way, so He's the only One who can make me more like Him. My only hope is to take my struggles to Jesus and ask Him to help me manage the tension between desires and distractions.

When I spend time with God, He challenges me to slow down and enjoy being with my husband and children. He knows how important they are to me, and He also knows how easily I get tangled up in my to-do list. He slows me down and gives me sweet reminders like my child's silhouette. He also helps me come up with creative ways to stay present with my people when my high-octane brain gets distracted.

- I look into their faces and remember what they used to look like. *This helps me grasp how quickly time flies.*
- I think back to what life was like without them. *This makes me thankful God gave them to me.*
- I imagine a day when they won't be with me, the day they may live in another city with their own families. *This makes me want to cry!* But then I freeze-frame that moment so it will last longer.
- I sometimes imagine it's the last time we will be together and focus on making it our best! *Yes, sometimes I have to go to that extreme.*

Time Slips Away

As my boys got older, school projects, friends, jobs, and extra-curricular activities filled their schedules, and we didn't get as much time with them. The more time slipped away, the more I wished I had spent less time on my computer and more time together when they were younger. During that season we decided to designate a family night each week so we could still have time together on a regular basis.

> The more time slipped away, the more I wished I had spent less time on my computer and more time together when they were younger.

We also started carving out margin in our schedules so J.J. and I could get one-on-one time with each of our kids to get to know them individually and do something together that they enjoyed. It wasn't weekly, but it was fairly regular for a season. J.J. rotated taking each of our boys to a different pizza place. Joshua and I usually went to the Barnes & Noble bookstore café, while Andrew liked going out to eat or watching a movie together.

Now that our boys are adults and no longer live at home, I am so grateful we made time together something we all enjoyed and looked forward to. That consistent time with our sons created a connection and traditions we still enjoy, even now that they are living on their own.

With Aster being our only child living at home, we are around each other a lot. But being around each other is not the same as planning time to be together. It's also hard to connect because meaningful conversations are difficult for her, but God has helped me find other creative ways to connect with Aster by entering her world through a door she is more comfortable with. She loves drawing pictures and coloring, playing with dolls, and showing me around the world of Roblox. Instead of getting frustrated that she loves being on her iPad, which is how I used to feel, I signed up for my own Roblox account so I could join her. And she loves it!

Simple Ways to Connect with Your Kids

- At dinner, or when you're getting the kids ready for bed, ask what the best and worst part of their day was. It is a great way to see into their hearts when their guard is down. (Be sure to bite your tongue and not offer advice or correction if their low includes something they got in trouble for at school or something you are tempted to react to.)
- Set five to ten minutes aside to spend with each child (or rotate between children each day) after school listening to the details of their day and offering to help with homework.
- Set aside a few minutes to do their favorite activity each week.
- Listen with undivided attention and watch how God opens a window in your kids' hearts that few get to look in.

Jesus valued face-to-face connections and surrounded Himself with family and friends—spending time with people over meals, at weddings, out fishing, and as they traveled together. Through His example, we see how important it is to satisfy our and our kids' craving for connection by spending time together!

Lord, You created us with a craving for connection and a sense of belonging that comes when we are together. In a digital world, it's easy to grow numb to our need for real-life relationships with screens pulling us away from what really matters. It's hard to know the balance of being together and getting things done. I need Your wisdom and direction as well as creative ideas my kids will enjoy. Help me remember, especially if they are resistant, that I am the parent, and with Your help we can find a way to build our relationships now so they are even stronger later. Amen.

fourteen

Your Child Needs to Know the Power of Prayer

I woke up at 2:15 a.m. and couldn't get back to sleep. My mind was tossing and turning with concerns and prayers for Joshua. He had been going through a difficult time, and my heart felt heavy for him. I had prayed for my son before I went to bed that night, asking Jesus to be real to him and to help Joshua navigate the hard parts of growing up. I fell asleep praying and woke up praying.

There have been many days and nights when my heart has been weighed down with concern for each of my children. I know I can't talk my children out of feeling the way they do. I can't deny, fix, or figure out what they are going through. I can't give them a few promises from the Bible and expect them to suddenly feel happy. The most important and most impactful thing I can do is pray for them and love them. And then pray some more.

Praying God's Promises for Our Children

One of the most powerful ways we can pray for our children is by praying God's promises for them. When we pray God's Word, we pray God's will. And when we pray God's will, 1 John 5:14 tells us, "This is the confidence we have in approaching God: that if we ask anything according to his will, he hears us." Also, when we pray God's will by praying God's Word, not only does He hear us, but He also moves nearer to us: "The LORD is near to all who call on him, to all who call on him in truth" (Ps. 145:18).

> One of the most powerful ways we can pray for our children is by praying God's promises for them.

When one of my children is going through something difficult, or if God prompts me to pray over an area of their life, I try to find verses related to what I am praying for and weave them into a prayer. Here are three Scripture prayers I've written to pray for my children, which cover three of the most important areas of our children's lives, no matter what age or stage they are in.

Growing Their Trust and Faith

Lord, I pray You would help _____ trust You with all their heart and lean not on their own understanding. I pray _____ would acknowledge You in all their ways and trust You to make their path straight. Lord, help _____ to live by faith and not by sight as they wait in hope for You, believing You are their help and shield. May Your unfailing love be with _____, Lord, as they learn how to put their hope in You. Amen (Prov. 3:5–6; 2 Cor. 5:7; Ps. 33:20, 22).

97

Guarding Their Hearts and Thoughts

Father, I pray You would help _____ guard their heart above all else, knowing it will determine the course of their life. Give _____ an awareness of their thoughts and remind _____ to take their thoughts captive and make sure they align with and are obedient to Yours. Lord, turn _____'s eyes from worthless things, and give _____ life through Your Word. Amen (Prov. 4:23 NLT; 2 Cor. 10:5; Ps. 119:37 NLT).

Guided by God's Voice and Truth

Lord, I pray You would speak to _____'s heart, and that You give _____ the ability to recognize Your voice and the desire to listen to and follow You. Show _____ Your ways, Lord, teach _____ Your paths. Guide _____ in Your truth and teach them, for You are their Savior. I pray _____ would put their hope in You all day long, and that Your Word would be a lamp to their feet and a light to their path. Amen (1 Sam. 3:10; John 10:27; Ps. 25:4–5; 119:105).

Find more Scriptures to pray for your kids at reneeswope.com /a-confident-mom/scripture-prayers.

A Legacy of Prayer

I didn't start learning about prayer until I was in my early twenties. And several years later, when I started having children, I was still learning. Maybe you are too. One of the things I struggled with was the pressure I felt to say the right things in the right way. I thought that if I prayed correctly, God would be more likely to listen and answer my prayers the way I wanted Him to. It took some time, but I realized these prayers were performance-based, which is a tendency of mine that shows up all over the place.

Thankfully, I got up the courage to talk to my mentor about it, and she assured me that "prayer isn't about saying or asking the right things, it's about building a relationship with God by talking to Him—and listening."[1] Her encouragement helped me take a deep breath and enjoy a more conversational approach to prayer, where I talked to God honestly and comfortably, the way I would with a friend or mentor.

I remember my baby-step beginnings of praying for Joshua during my pregnancy. My prayers were simple. I wanted my child to experience Jesus's peace and protection. As time passed and my relationship with God grew, so did my desire to leave a legacy of prayer by creating patterns of prayer in our everyday lives.

Covered in Prayer

From the time our kids were infants, we have covered them in prayer before bedtime. Initially, bedtime prayers were my way of entrusting my babies to Jesus to keep them safe and calm, and help them sleep so I could too.

As our children got older, we continued our tradition of praying over them as they fell asleep, using our prayers to remind them of God's love and protection. We also hoped our prayers would help them get comfortable talking to God themselves one day and would remind them He would be watching over them all night long.

Andrew recently told me our praying over him as he fell asleep is one of the biggest things he remembers about prayer from his childhood. He said he was afraid to go to sleep sometimes because he thought we might leave our house once he and Joshua were in bed. But when we prayed over him, it gave him peace and assurance and helped him fall asleep. Aster said she likes when we pray for her too, but sometimes it feels weird because she can't see God.

Gathered in Prayer

When I started writing this chapter, I couldn't remember if we ever deliberately sat down with our boys to talk about prayer. I wondered if either of them remembered us teaching them about prayer, so I called Joshua and Andrew to ask what, if anything, they remembered learning about prayer at home (not at church or youth group). I kind of held my breath, knowing they may not recall a thing.

Neither of them were prepared for my phone call or my question, and had to think for a minute. But then I got a surprising gift. Although they weren't together when I asked, they both mentioned a couple of the same things. One of the biggest of these was how we would regularly gather together as a family to pray. Joshua said that felt like a big part of how we raised them and that it was a constant from the time they were little all the way through high school, and even now.

We started inviting our kids to pray with us when they were two or three years old. These weren't planned but rather were spontaneous "Hey, let's ask God to _____" prayers. We prayed about everything from gas grills that wouldn't start to what to do about tires stolen off J.J.'s car, school decisions, vacation wishes, a baby sister from Africa, a grandma in the hospital, and a gazillion other things.

We wanted our children to be part of asking and watching for God's answers, hoping this might help them see God's presence and participation in our lives and theirs. We also wanted them to be aware that we live in a spiritual realm as much as a physical realm. And we wanted them to know prayer is a conversation we can have with God anytime about anything, because He is someone we trust and depend on. Someone we can go to for directions and making decisions or to talk to about our desires and concerns for others.

Protected by Prayer

Joshua and Andrew told me another thing they remember learning while growing up was about the protection of prayer.

Andrew said that because he heard us pray so much, he knew prayer was part of who we were and what we did, and that gave him a sense of protection because he knew we'd also pray for him when he wasn't with us.

Joshua remembers us teaching him how to pray and claim Scripture to protect his mind and overcome darkness when dealing with spiritual attacks. Sadly, he first learned that lesson when he was only six or seven years old. One night he came to me with a terrified look on his face and said, "I can't get to sleep because I keep hearing voices in my head telling me to kill myself."

Shocked and concerned, I asked a few questions and noticed Joshua was not thinking *I want to kill myself* but rather was hearing, "Kill yourself."

This was clearly a spiritual attack, and I was mama-bear furious. That night we prayed Scripture out loud over our little boy, boldly claiming the truth that Joshua was a child of God, holy and dearly loved with God's fierce and perfect love that casts out fear (John 1:12, Col. 3:12, 1 John 4:18). We explained that God tells us to fight with "the sword of the Spirit, which is the word of God. And pray in the Spirit . . . with all kinds of prayers and requests" (Eph. 6:17–18). Joshua said that ever since then he's memorized and used God's Word as a weapon, and he has seen how speaking and praying Scripture out loud is the most powerful protection.

Living and Leaving a Legacy of Prayer

Although I wasn't sure we had talked enough with our children about the subject of prayer, God graciously filled in the gaps of what we didn't do and used what we did. And I am confident He will do the same for you.

God created your children on purpose and with purpose! He invites you to join Him through prayer in the work He has begun and promises to complete in their lives. You don't have to know a whole lot to make a big difference with your prayers. Your words don't have to be poignant or grammatically perfect. What matters most is that you pray for and with your children, knowing that "you can leave a legacy for generations to come. Your prayers have the power to shape the destiny of your children and your children's children."[2]

Lord, I want my children to experience Your presence and Your participation in our lives. I pray that You would remind me to cover my children in prayer, gather them in prayer, and protect them in prayer as I create a home and a life where talking to You is a constant. I want prayer to be a natural part of what we do, not only at mealtimes and bedtimes but throughout our day. I pray that our prayers would form a pattern in our family, building a legacy that will continue in my children's lives and in their families for generations to come. Amen.

fifteen

Your Child Needs to Be Equipped for Life's Battles

When Andrew was eight years old, he walked into my bathroom before school one morning and declared, "Mom, I don't want to have *any* anxious thoughts today! I don't want to worry about you not being home when I get off the school bus. I don't want to worry about my teacher not liking my science project. And I don't want to worry about Dad getting in a car accident! I wish I could be like other kids because they never worry."

My heart sank as I listened to Andrew describe worries and fears he had obviously been fighting on a daily basis. This was the first time Andrew had told me about the thoughts that waged war in his mind, and I was really glad he had come to me. I had battled anxiety and fear since I was a child, so I knew just how lonely, overwhelmed, and frustrated he felt. But I was also surprised, because I had assumed my fears had stemmed from my unstable childhood and trauma from my homelife.

For years, I'd accepted my battle with fear and worry as a war I couldn't win because I didn't think I had enough ammunition to beat them or enough authority to overpower their attacks. But that had been changing as I studied Scripture and discovered there was a bigger battle going on. My struggle wasn't just circumstantial or emotional. It was not "against flesh and blood, but against the rulers, against the authorities, against the powers of this dark world and against the spiritual forces of evil in the heavenly realms" (Eph. 6:12).

I was not helpless! I had access to spiritual ammunition and authority in Christ. So did my eight-year-old son who had just declared he wanted a day off from his war with worry, and I was determined to help him get it.

Empowering Our Children with Spiritual Truth

While I listened to Andrew describe what he had been dealing with, I asked Jesus to show me what to do and what to say. Although I wanted to take Andrew's battle with worry away, I knew I couldn't. What I could do was go to war with him in prayer and equip him with God's truth to face his fears courageously and fight them victoriously.

> What I could do was go to war with him in prayer and equip him with God's truth to face his fears courageously and fight them victoriously.

These words from Scripture came to mind: "For though we live in the world, we do not wage war as the world does. The weapons we fight with are not the weapons of the world. On the contrary, they have divine power to demolish strongholds" (2 Cor. 10:3–4).

And that is when I knew what to say. I told Andrew, "You have the power to decide what to do with your worries." And then I shared these three important truths with him:

Truth #1: You are not alone. Other kids worry too; they just don't talk about it with friends.

Truth #2: You are not weak or weird. Worry and fear are a normal struggle. Otherwise, God would not tell us what to do with them more than a hundred times in the Bible.

Truth #3: You are not powerless. God tells us what to do with worries when they come!

Next, I grabbed my Bible and read this verse to Andrew: "We demolish arguments and every pretension that sets itself up against the knowledge of God, and we take captive every thought to make it obedient to Christ" (v. 5).

The puzzled look on his face told me he needed to know how to do that, so I described it in terms he could understand. "Andrew, when you have a thought that makes you feel anxious, you have to decide to catch it like a baseball." I then cupped my hand like I was holding a ball and told him to look at it and ask, "Is this something Jesus would say to me?" If the answer was no, then he could throw that thought back into the outfield!

For instance, worry says, "Your mom isn't going to be home when you get off the bus."

"Would Jesus say that to you?" I asked.

"No," he replied.

"Then it's outta here!" I told him, as I threw the invisible ball across the room.

Worry says, "Your teacher isn't going to like your science project!"

"Would Jesus say that?" I prompted.

"No."

"Throw that one away too!"

We talked through each worry, and I helped him decide what to do. Then we prayed and asked God to replace each worry with confident peace, and thanked God for ways He'd protected Andrew in the past, reminding Andrew how good He is at being God.

After our collective amen, I looked up to see that Andrew had a big grin on his face. Then he said, "Thanks, Mom!" as though all his worries were gone.

Equipping Our Children with Practical Tools

Our kids need us to be available to talk through their battles, listen to their stories, pray through their struggles, and share God's truths that help us face ours. And, just like us, they need practical tools to help them apply God's truths. For instance, we can share with our children that God tells us,

> Cast all your anxiety on him because he cares for you. (1 Pet. 5:7)

> Do not be anxious about anything, but in everything by prayer and supplication with thanksgiving let your requests be made known to God. And the peace of God, which surpasses all understanding, will guard your hearts and your minds in Christ Jesus. (Phil. 4:6–7 ESV)

Then, we can show them how to cast their cares on Jesus.

- On a piece of paper, have your child write cares and concerns they can't stop thinking or worrying about.
- Put the piece(s) of paper in an envelope.
- On the outside of the envelope, have them write "Jesus, I give my cares and concerns to You because You care about me."
- Have your child put the envelope in their Bible or your Bible, say a prayer telling God about their concerns and worries, and then thank Him for three to five things He has done in the past to take care of them and these concerns. Ask Jesus for peace to replace the worries and for courage to trust Him.

- Explain that worrying is basically thinking about something over and over, but it doesn't change anything. God is the only One who can take care of the things we think and worry about. Make a commitment to carry these concerns to God as you pray for them each day for the next week, and tell them to come back if their concerns return and go through the process again and again.

We may want to fight our children's battles for them or be tempted to fix their problems and ease difficult situations. But solving their problems or fighting their battles isn't what they need. What they need are powerful truths and practical tools that will empower and equip them with the ability to navigate life's battles when we aren't there while pointing them to the One who will always be with them.

Lord, thank You for being the One who goes to battle for us and with us. Sometimes I forget that part of my role as a mom is to equip my children for the battles they will face in life, and that they have an enemy who is going to attack them with fear, worry, discouragement, and more. But I don't have to be afraid. You are my Commander and their Defender, and in Christ we have victory. I pray my children would come to me with their concerns, confident I will not judge them but pray for them. Help me walk in Your truth so I can share Your Word and show my kids how to lean on You when they come to me. Amen.

sixteen

Your Child Needs to Be Disciplined in Love

One afternoon, Andrew came to me with tears streaming down his hot red cheeks. When I asked what was wrong, he said our dachshund, Chelsea, bit him. Chelsea had never bitten anyone before, and I had a feeling she wouldn't do that unless she felt threatened. I asked a few questions and eventually Andrew told me Chelsea bit him after he hit and poked her with his plastic sword. I was tempted to tell him I probably would've bitten him too, but I held that thought.

As I mentioned earlier, although I shifted my focus to noticing and nurturing the gold of God's character in my kids, I still needed to deal with the dirt of those not-so-golden attitudes and actions, like being mean, selfish, argumentative, disobedient, and more.

So, I'd added a column to our character chart with the heading "Dirt That Buries the Gold." In that column I listed actions and attitudes that were the opposite of the character traits we were learning. That way, in situations like this one, instead of just correcting Andrew by telling him to be kind to the dog, I could use our character chart for teaching and redirecting him.

I pulled out the chart and we looked in that column for behaviors that represented the dirt of hitting a dog with a sword: being mean, uncaring, and selfish sounded like a good fit. These traits were listed as the dirt (sin) that buries the gold of kindness.

> I still needed to deal with the dirt of those not-so-golden attitudes and actions, like being mean, selfish, argumentative, disobedient, and more.

We read our definition of kindness: "being nice to people (and pets) in our thoughts and actions," and the verse that goes with it, Ephesians 4:32, "Be kind to one another [and] tenderhearted" (ESV). Afterward I explained to Andrew how being mean is the opposite of showing kindness and asked him to tell me three ways he could be kind to Chelsea.

The Gospel of Dirt

Have you ever tried to explain sin to your kids? I have found sin is hard for adults to understand, much less children. But when I explained to my boys how sin is like the dirt that buries gold, they seemed to grasp the concept a little better. As we learned more and more about God's character and I referred to the "dirt" when disciplining our kids, I always pointed out how sin, like dirt, covers the image of God in us, which is why we need Jesus to take our sins away.

As our children got a little older, we explained what happened in the garden with Adam and Eve and helped them put the pieces together about why their sin hurt God's heart and separated them from Him. We talked about how the whole Bible is about God pursuing His children, because He wants to restore them back into relationship with Him. This helped our children realize they needed a Savior to forgive them of their sins so that they would not be defined by the dirt. It created a path for us to walk with them to the foot of the cross and show them God's grace through the forgiveness and sacrifice of Jesus.

Our kids didn't quickly understand why Jesus had to die on the cross for their sins. Honestly, as an adult it took me a long time to really grasp it too. But the word picture of mining for gold gave us a way to help our kids begin to understand why it matters.

The Discipleship of Discipline

The word *discipline* comes from the root word *disciple*, which means one who is a follower of a teacher or one who is a student. Jesus taught His disciples and us that the greatest command is to love God and love others (Matt. 22:37–39). At the heart of discipleship and discipline, we teach our kids how to take responsibility for their choices, treat others with respect, and seek restoration in relationships when their choices have caused damage.

> An important part of disciplining our children is teaching them how to make good choices now that will help them make wise decisions later, choices that honor God, other people, and their furry friends.

An important part of disciplining our children is teaching them how to make good choices now that will help them make wise decisions later, choices that honor God, other people, and their furry friends.

Lord, thank You for the analogy of gold mining and the parallel of dirt that can help me teach my children about sin. When they do something that does not reflect Your heart, in their attitude or action, I pray You would help me choose not to react but instead to act on what I am learning by using it as a teachable moment. Help me talk to them about the choice they made and the choice they could have made that reflects Your character in them. Amen.

seventeen

Your Child Needs to Be Forgiven and Restored

We'd spent the day swimming with my friend Vicki and her kids, and since our husbands were out of town together, I invited Vicki and her kids to come over for dinner. When they arrived, I was putting hot dogs and hamburgers on the grill, baked beans were almost ready, and crispy French fries would be coming out of the oven in fifteen minutes. The kids played together while Vicki and I chatted and set the table.

Suddenly, I heard a horrible scream with a pitch that told me someone was seriously injured. I ran to see what happened and found Joshua balled up on our living room floor, crying and screaming, "Andrew bit me!"

Andrew stood there stuttering and blaming Joshua because he wouldn't give him a turn with a toy. I'm sure Joshua was at fault too, but biting ranked up there as an "unforgivable sin" in our house, so I didn't care why he did it in that moment.

I lifted Joshua's shirt and saw a large, bright red bite mark on his hip. I felt infuriated and equally embarrassed that my child would do something like that.

Breathe and Count to Ten

I told Andrew to go to the bathroom and shut the door and wait for me. Just as I was ready to march in to discipline him, I had a check in my spirit. *Wait. Do not discipline in anger. Calm down before you correct him. Breathe and count to ten.*

Although taking care of Joshua should've been my first priority, my anger with Andrew had my blood boiling, and my focus had zoomed in on his consequences. I needed to step back and look at the situation from a wider angle.

It's crazy how a mama's mind can assess several different situations, in detail, all at the same time: I was trying to figure out what I needed to do to make sure Joshua didn't get an infection while thinking about how horrified Vicki and her kids must be and also trying to come up with the worst punishment possible for Andrew. I was also afraid Vicki would think Andrew might bite one of her kids. I'd heard of friendships ending over a biting child, which made me even more determined to make sure this never happened again.

Once Joshua's wound was clean and covered, and we were both calm, I knew it was now time to take corrective measures with Andrew. The Lord reminded me it was Andrew's heart that needed to be dealt with, and his actions would follow.

I got him out of the bathroom and walked with him upstairs to his room, away from everyone else. He cried the whole way up and continued as we sat in a rocking chair in his room.

I looked him in the eyes and asked him why he bit Joshua. I also asked him if he had felt angry, and he said he did. He tried to explain, and I just listened.

When he was done, I explained that animals bite, but not people. He broke down sobbing and said, "Mommy, I just want to pray."

"Okay," I said, "you pray first."

"God, please take the bad stuff out of my heart," he said. Then he looked up and told me, "I forgot what else to say."

I helped him along, and he finished by telling God, "I am sorry I bit Joshua. Please forgive me, and please help me never do that again."

Afterward he looked at me through fresh tears and muttered, "I'm such a bad person. I do such bad things. I have so much dirt in my heart!"

Teachable Moments

My anger had melted away, and now my heart ached as I listened to Andrew's self-condemning thoughts. I knew this could be a valuable teachable moment. I wanted to help Andrew see himself and his sin separately.

So I told him, "Andrew, you are not a bad person. I've seen you be kind and compassionate. I've seen how thoughtful you can be. But today you chose to bite Joshua because you were angry. That is what you did, but it is not who you are. You are a child of God. You are my child, Andrew Nathan Swope, and did you know Nathan means 'gift of God'? You are God's gift to me, and I love you! I may not like what you do, but I will always love you!"

As I held Andrew, my long list of potential consequences scrolled through my thoughts. I had decided he would eat dinner by himself upstairs and go to bed early, but should I also put soap in his mouth, take away screen time for a week, television for two weeks, and take all his favorite toys away too?

These were the options I'd come up with earlier. Now I didn't know what to do, so I asked God to show me. For the first time in my seven years of parenting, God brought to my mind the story of the prodigal son in Luke 15:11–32. I thought about how the father responded when his younger son repented and turned back toward home. He ran to his son with arms wide open and welcomed him back home and back into his arms. As the image of a forgiving father holding his repentant son came to mind, I sensed God whispering to my soul, *Invite him back to the table.*

It almost took my breath away. That was so far from what I had been thinking, but I knew it was exactly what Jesus would do. Reaching out my hand to hold Andrew's, I invited him to come with me back downstairs to eat dinner. He went over to the living room where the kids were playing and told Joshua he was sorry. Joshua said he forgave him, and they hugged.

Vicki was setting up our dinner assembly line on the kitchen counter with hot dogs, hamburgers, and all the yummy side items so it'd be easy to serve the kids and ourselves. I smiled at her, and we both let out a big sigh. As I pulled paper plates out of our pantry and went to put them on the counter, Jesus whispered again to my soul, *Serve Andrew first.*

I almost started crying right then and there. God's grace overwhelms me and humbles me. His desire was immediate restoration of Andrew's relationship with Joshua and with me. He wanted me to see that His purpose for discipline is not to create regret. The purpose of God's discipline is to restore us back into relationship with Him and with others.

> His purpose for discipline is not to create regret. The purpose of God's discipline is to restore us back into relationship with Him and with others.

Andrew had no idea God spared him from much worse punishment that night. And he didn't notice he was served dinner first. But I knew. It was me God was speaking to. It was me He was changing. That night He showed me the depth of His tender mercy and lavish grace. It was so far from what I'd seen or experienced in my childhood. It was my heart He was healing. And I would never be the same.

God wanted me (and He wants you) to see His heart of grace and mercy. He is not angry or disappointed. He is loving, patient, and kind. He forgives, holds, pursues, and invites us back to the table, again and again.

Relationship-Driven Parenting

As I grew in my understanding of godly discipline and grace, I wanted my kids to understand the importance of restoring relationships damaged through hurtful choices. So, I started teaching them to go back to the person they offended and say, "I'm sorry, will you forgive me?"

I also wanted them to learn to say "I forgive you" when someone apologized to them. That was important to me, because God didn't just say, "It's okay," to us. He said, "I forgive you," which means our debt has been canceled. I wanted my kids to understand that forgiveness cancels the debt and restores broken relationships by building a bridge between us. If I didn't teach our children how to apologize and forgive, how would they understand their own need for forgiveness or grasp the redemptive work God accomplished through Jesus for them?

Early on my tendency was to punish my kids so they'd never misbehave the same way again, but I realized that day God doesn't do that with us. He doesn't try to scare us out of doing bad things. He looks at our hearts and addresses our sin issues with the intention of changing us from the inside out. His goal is restoration, not regret. His desire is to draw us close, back into relationship with Him.

Relationship-driven parenting needs to be our goal when it comes to disciplining our children in love. It focuses on restoring the relationship that has been broken and applying the grace of forgiveness to mend hurts and bring hearts back together, and in doing so we show our kids how important it is to restore broken relationships with others and God.

Jesus, what a picture of radical grace You give us. You were willing to be completely separated from God so we didn't have to be. You extended Your arms on the cross and welcomed us home. You invited us to the table and gave us a place of honor we did nothing to deserve. When I'm afraid You're mad at me, remind me to turn toward You because You will be there waiting with open arms to welcome me. And then, help me live out a boundary setting yet boundless kind of love with my children, as I receive it from You. Amen.

eighteen

Your Child Needs Clear Boundaries, Choices, Consequences, and Consistency

❧

Do you remember getting in trouble as a kid? I remember getting a spanking when I was younger and being sent to my room, where I lay in my bed and cried. Eventually my tears stopped and the sting on my bottom wore off, but my heart hurt for the rest of the day. Mom was still angry with me, and it felt like a brick wall had gone up between us.

I hated that feeling of separation and not knowing how long it would take for Mom to let me back in. Apologies and forgiveness were never mentioned in our home, which meant conflicts and consequences left our relationships fractured. That is what happens when we commit an offense against someone or against God: it fractures the relationship and separates us.

But what is so amazing about God is that His grace and forgiveness, offered through Jesus, mend brokenness and build a bridge between our hearts so we don't have to work our way back into His presence again.

Although J.J. and I don't always get it right, loving discipline has been a high priority in our parenting and an area we try to approach with intention and patience. We realize discipline and correction can cause a lot of damage if not handled wisely and prayerfully. We also know a loving, biblical approach to discipline can lead to some of the most important heart-shaping and character-developing conversations parents can have with their kids.

So, how do we balance loving our children and disciplining them? In Proverbs 13:24, God says we *love* our children when we discipline them. In Genesis 2–3, God shows us what loving discipline looks like through His parenting approach with Adam and Eve. He gave them clear boundaries and the freedom of choice. He also communicated consequences if they didn't obey, and He was consistent in following through. These four elements are a great blueprint for loving biblical discipline.

> A loving, biblical approach to discipline can lead to some of the most important heart-shaping and character-developing conversations parents can have with their kids.

Clear Boundaries

Just like God did with Adam and Eve, we need to love our children by taking the time to define clear boundaries. We also need to tell our kids what the boundaries are before they cross them and the consequences of going outside of them. And then we need to love our kids enough to stick with what we said and follow through if they step out of the boundaries we have communicated.

119

Choices

By giving children a choice, we empower them to take responsibility for their decisions. If children are taught how to take responsibility for their choices, they will grow up knowing their actions make a difference, good or bad. Galatians 6:4 says, "Each one should test their own actions. Then they can take pride in themselves."

Choices also give children a sense of independence and control. They can choose to obey, or they can choose to be disciplined. It's up to them! When we are in a situation and one of our kids is on the edge of a boundary we set, we need to tell them, "You have a choice. Either you choose to stop _____ or you choose the consequence of _____. You get to choose."

Consequences

Although it is easier to react and decide in the heat of the moment what we are going to threaten to do if our kids step out of bounds, that is confusing for our children. It doesn't create the safety and certainty they need. It also sets us up to discipline in anger, which damages our relationship and leaves us feeling guilty about it later. The best way to guide our children is to plan ahead (as much as possible) and communicate what the consequences will be if one of our children does something that crosses a boundary we've set (e.g., being disrespectful, arguing, hitting).

When our children choose to go outside of the boundaries we have set, we need to stick to our words (like God did) and allow them to experience the consequences of their choices. It is not mean or harsh—it's biblical discipline, which is an act of love.

Consistency

When we do what we tell our children we are going to do, it helps our kids respect us. Consistency also builds trust and security.

Home becomes a safe place to take risks and test the boundaries. A parent who is consistent in doing what they say is not being "the worst parent ever" but is actually teaching their children they can be trusted.

Disciplining our children consistently takes time plus a whole lot of patience and effort. It's easy to avoid giving consequences for bad behavior because it takes us away from what we want to be doing, like talking to a friend, cooking dinner, or trying to get ready to go somewhere. But it's so important. Our kids argued and complained so much less when they knew I would keep my promise on what I told them the consequences would be.

Guiding Principles

It's important as a parent to prayerfully determine your guiding principles when it comes to discipline. That way you have a plan in place that will help you respond in love rather than react in anger. Here are our eight guiding principles for disciplining our children in love:

1. We discipline our children in private, away from anyone else involved.

2. We wait until our emotions and our child's emotions are calm before we discuss the situation or discipline the child.

3. We ask what happened and address the choices they made. We also ask them what they could have done differently that would have led to a better result.

4. Before we talk about consequences, we communicate unconditional love.

5. We remind them that God calls us as their parents to discipline them in love and to teach them to make choices that honor other people, themselves, and God.

6. After we give them their consequences, we hug them and express our love for them again.

7. We always tell our child that we believe in them and that their behavior is not who they are but something they chose to do.

8. If someone else was involved in the situation, we ask them to apologize and ask forgiveness from the person they hurt.

From Their Perspective

While writing these chapters, I decided to ask Andrew and Joshua their perspectives on our approach to discipline. I had no idea what they would say, but I am glad I asked, because their answers gave us insights into how Aster may feel as well. Here are our boys' responses:

> I needed to know the difference between right and wrong, but I was almost always convinced I was right. So, it helped that you and Dad took time to talk with us before you disciplined us. You asked me if I knew why I was in trouble to get me to name what I did, then you'd ask why I did it. It made me feel heard and it helped me realize why it was wrong. I'm honestly glad you guys disciplined me when I did something wrong, but also told me what I could have done differently. —Joshua, 26

> I appreciated that you guys didn't hold grudges. You may have been angry one day, but you weren't still mad at me the next day. You really forgave me, and I could tell. It also meant a lot that when I was in trouble, you took me into another room and didn't correct me in front of people. It was important to me to be treated with respect, especially if my friends were around. You didn't do that perfectly, but you got better at it as I got older. Your actions matched your words. You didn't just say you loved us, you guys acted like you loved us, even when no one else was around. —Andrew, 23

Shaping Hearts, Not Just Habits

It is so important that we correct our children lovingly and use discipline as an opportunity to shape their hearts, not just their habits. Loving, biblical discipline with all three of our children has opened the door to some of the most important conversations we've had. Those conversations about their choices, along with consequences and our best effort at consistency, all laid a foundation our children could build on for the rest of their lives.

> It is so important that we correct our children lovingly and use discipline as an opportunity to shape their hearts, not just their habits.

The best way to cultivate a culture at home that is conducive to this approach is to start by creating a positive learning experience in a loving environment where encouragement, relationship, unconditional love, and nurtured character are core values. That way, when times of discipline come, a healthy foundation will already be in place where our children trust us and know we truly love them and want the best for them.

Lord, thank You for showing us what loving discipline looks like through Your parenting approach with Adam and Eve. Help me define clear boundaries for my kids, knowing they need the freedom of choice and predetermined consequences if they cross the boundaries I have set. Help me be consistent in following through on what I said, knowing that discipline will help my children learn how to make good choices as they grow up. Remind me to approach discipline with love, intention, and patience, and to see it as an opportunity for heart-shaping and character-developing conversations with them. Amen.

nineteen

Your Child Needs to Know the Real Hero of Every Bible Story

❧

When I surrendered my life to Christ in my early twenties and started reading my Bible, almost every story was new to me. However, friends of mine could name their favorite Bible characters before they were even potty trained. They grew up going to vacation Bible school and church camps and had the books of the Bible memorized. Sometimes when they talked about Bible characters, I thought they were talking about family members.

I knew nothing about David, Ruth, Jonah, Martha, or Moses. And the only Joseph I'd heard of was Jesus's stepdad (at least that is how I saw him), but I was a little confused about his colorful coat because it had never been mentioned in the Christmas stories I'd read. I didn't know who in the world a tiny little man named Zacchaeus was or the dead man they called Lazarus. Both sounded to me like characters an adult might dress up as for Halloween or Mardi Gras.

Did I mention I grew up Catholic and lived in New Orleans until I was twelve years old? My parents were divorced and took us to church mainly on Easter and Christmas. That might help you understand why I was biblically confused. I knew very little about God, Jesus, the Holy Spirit, and important people in the Bible. Since then, especially once our boys started going to Sunday school, I have learned a lot about them.

But I noticed a difference between what I was learning in my Bible studies and what my children were learning in Sunday school. In my boys' Sunday school classes, the hero was always the main character of a story, a man or woman who was brave, strong, obedient, or kind. Oftentimes details about the hero's flaws and failures were left out.

For instance, most children's storybook Bibles don't mention that Moses killed someone. Or the fact that after the flood and God's rainbow promise, Noah drank too much alcohol and his sons found him naked. King David committed adultery and arranged to have the woman's husband killed.

The Powerful Truth

I know those details aren't age-appropriate for young children, which is why they are taught a G-rated version. But here's what I also know: as an adult, I had the advantage of reading those stories for the first time with all of the details included, and they made my jaw drop! Not because I was shocked by what these chosen influencers and leaders had done; instead, I was dumbfounded by God's grace and mercy and completely blown away by His kindness and faithfulness, not theirs.

Knowing everything about them and Him convinced me that God's love really was unconditional. Jesus really was a Savior, in more ways

Jesus was relatable, ridiculously patient, kind, forgiving, and fun. Seeing how Jesus treated people made me feel like I could be myself with Him.

than one! And although He was perfect, His perfection wasn't intimidating. He didn't make people feel like He was better than them. He was relatable, ridiculously patient, kind, forgiving, and fun. Seeing how Jesus treated people made me feel like I could be myself with Him. The more I got to know God—the Father, Son, and Holy Spirit—as the hero of every Bible story, the more I wanted Him to be the hero of my story. And that is what our kids need!

Inspired by Imperfection

At some point, before they are teenagers, our kids need and deserve to know who the real hero is of every story in the Bible. And I think parents (not Sunday school teachers or youth group leaders) are the most important influencers in their lives, which makes us the best people to tell them. We are the ones who will know when our children are ready to hear the PG and PG-13 version of the Bible. We can explain why those details weren't included in their toddler Bibles and why we are telling them now.

Do we still talk about and emphasize the great qualities and character traits of typical biblical heroes? Yes, absolutely. We and our children should still be inspired by these men and women who had great faith even though it wasn't perfect, had courage that sometimes wavered, and chose to trust God in very difficult situations even though they'd doubted Him the day before. Some didn't have the strengths or qualifications they needed, but God accepted and approved of them just as they were.

When pointing out how very normal and in need of God those heroic men and women were, the goal is to emphasize how very imperfect we all are, yet God still loves us, chooses us, and uses us. It is because of Him that these people were willing to take risks and were able to do great things.

And on those days when your children are struggling with self-doubt or comparing themselves to someone else, pull out your Bible and read about one of the unqualified and imperfect people God chose to use to do important things for Him. And be sure they notice how God never said, "Well, you're not like_____, so I can't use you," to any one of them. Here is a list of my favorites:

Jacob was a cheater.

David was a murderer.

Mary was young.

Gideon was afraid.

Peter was a liar.

Martha was anxious.

Moses was insecure.

Paul hated Jesus.

Jonah hated the Ninevites.

Sarah was impatient.

Abraham was really old.

Naomi was bitter.

Thomas was a doubter.

Miriam was a gossip.

Lazarus was dead.

I love how God loves to use imperfect, inadequate, ordinary people to do extraordinary things. His power shows up strongest in our weakness because that is when we are most dependent on Him. The same thing the Lord said to Paul, He says to us today: "My grace is sufficient for you, for my power is made perfect in weakness" (2 Cor. 12:9).

God wants our kids to know it's okay—and perfectly normal—to be imperfect. He would love to be the hero of their story too.

Lord, I want my children to know that YOU are the hero of every Bible story. Thank You for men and women in the Bible we can learn from and look up to because of their character and their love for You and others. But I want to point my children to You, more than anyone else, as the true hero of our story. Give me discernment to know when my children are ready to hear the mature details and more complex issues of many Bible stories so they will see how gracious You are and how much You lavish love and honor on imperfect people who love and follow You. Amen.

twenty

Your Child Needs a Safe Place to Question Their Faith

When Joshua was three and a half, he started asking questions about death, cemeteries, and Jesus. He also wanted to know how electricity got into those little holes in the wall that he wasn't supposed to touch. I wasn't sure how to navigate explaining salvation, electricity, or cemeteries to a toddler.

I sensed Joshua getting close to wanting to invite Jesus into his heart. I knew I should be happy about that, but in the back of my mind, I struggled with what it would look like for Joshua to make a commitment to Christ at such a young age. I knew so many people who gave their life to Christ at a younger age and later questioned if the decision was theirs or their parents' or only the result of their being in a youth group. I couldn't count how many people I'd met who grew up in a Christian home and then went through a hard season of questioning if their salvation was ever real.

I wanted Joshua to give his heart to Jesus, but I feared he would doubt his salvation one day. I gave my life to Jesus in my twenties and experienced life change as I walked out of darkness into His light. I never questioned if it was real, and I wanted my children to have that same confidence in their relationship with Christ.

But . . . God

I talked to God about my concerns, sharing how I wanted Joshua to be old enough to understand his decision and remember it as an adult. Then, once I got quiet, I clearly sensed God telling me not to get in His way. It wasn't audible but it was clear and convicting as these thoughts crossed my mind: *Do not put your fears in between Me and Joshua. Trust Me with his story.*

With a lump in my throat, I surrendered my fears, my timeline, and my little boy to God. A few days later, I was loading the dishwasher and Joshua was eating a peanut butter and jelly sandwich when he casually announced, "Mommy, I want to invite Jesus into my heart. Right now."

"Okay," I replied as I walked over to him and wiped crumbs off the tablecloth. I explained to Joshua what that meant and told him he could repeat a prayer I would say to guide him. We bowed our heads at our kitchen table, and my little guy gave his heart to Jesus.

About two years later, while J.J. and I were out of town, we called my mom, who was keeping our boys, to see how everything was going. My mom said, "Well, I think Joshua is going to be a preacher. He just drew a picture of three crosses on a hill and told Andrew he needs to ask Jesus into his heart." Andrew did what his big brother told him and repeated the prayer Joshua said. Now we had two little guys who had given their hearts to Jesus.

Between ages nine and ten, both boys decided individually (two years apart) to get baptized and recommit their lives to Christ. They each had a different experience that prompted their decision without our influence. I wish I could tell you both boys followed Jesus with all their hearts from that point forward, but that's not what happened. The fact is both of our boys had a faith crisis when they were in their early teens.

Creating a Safe Place to Ask Hard Questions

When Joshua and Andrew walked away from God between ages fourteen and fifteen, our world was shattered to the core both times. Somehow, we didn't panic in front of them. J.J. and I calmly asked them questions to help us understand. But later, when we were alone in our bedroom closet, we let all of our feelings, questions, anger, fears, and concerns come out. More than once, with each other and with God.

Our number one priority was to keep our relationship with them close and to make home a safe place where they could ask hard questions. We also wanted our home to be a place where they felt accepted and respected as individuals, listened to, and loved.

We were devastated, but we were also glad they were still living at home when this happened. Although we had no idea what to say or do, we sensed our attitude and actions were more important than our words.

We prayed God's promises for them but decided not to push the Bible or our beliefs on them. They had heard both their whole lives. This needed to be their decision. If we said too much or pushed too hard, we would push them away, and that was the last thing we wanted to do.

Feeling Like a Failure

J.J. struggled with feeling like a failure. But strangely, I didn't feel like we'd failed. All those years before, God had somehow shifted my focus away from success versus failure and put a desire in my heart to simply be faithful.

By God's grace, I felt like we had been faithful. We were not perfect, not even close. But in the midst of our imperfect parenting, we'd done our best to fill our home and our kids' hearts with God's Word and our days with His presence by seeking Him and inviting Him into our ordinary, everyday lives.

> Some days, admitting we messed up and apologizing to our kids was the best we had to offer.

Some days, admitting we messed up and apologizing to our kids was the best we had to offer, but it was more than I'd ever received from my parents. And it felt like, in God's eyes, that was enough on those days. I tried to remind J.J. of all of these things and encourage him that he had been a great dad and still was.

Fear versus Faith

Failure didn't sink me, but fear tried to take me down. I was afraid of how far Andrew might go and how dark things might get. I come from a family filled with alcoholism and other addictions, and I feared he would make choices that would lead him into bondage and deep regret.

One afternoon Andrew and I were driving home from school, and I was talking to him about my concerns. I told Andrew I wasn't going to push him toward God, but I was going to pull him away from darkness if I saw him getting too close. When I stopped talking, Andrew said, "Mom, if you believe God is as strong and powerful as you always told me He was, then you wouldn't be afraid."

He was right. My faith was being tested like never before. That afternoon when we got home, I went to my room and cried. I told Jesus I did believe, and I cried out to Him in my unbelief. I was desperate to see Him work in ways only He could, and a season of parenting that almost crushed me also strengthened me.

Joshua and Andrew both came to their own conclusion that God the Father, Son, and Holy Spirit are real, and they surrendered their hearts and their lives to Him late in their teen years. It wasn't because we said the right things or took away all the bad things. That was so much more than we could see or do. However, I believe the most important thing we did was let them find their own faith and find their own way to the heart of God.

> When I stopped talking, Andrew said, "Mom, if you believe God is as strong and powerful as you always told me He was, then you wouldn't be afraid."

If you'd like to know more about Andrew's and Josh's faith stories, and our journey with them, I share more details at reneeswope .com/a-confident-mom/faith.

Doing Things the Same and Differently

When our sons became young adults, we asked them what it was like growing up in a Christian home. Both Joshua and Andrew said that hearing about Jesus dying on the cross their whole life made it so familiar it lost its significance. It didn't impact them the way they wish it had as teenagers. One of them said when the gospel was shared, it started sounding like Charlie Brown's teacher: *wah, wah wah, wah, wah* . . . and they kind of tuned out.

But Andrew did say that all of the songs we sang about Jesus and how much God loves them, all throughout their childhood, came back and played in "stereo" in his head the whole time he was an atheist. He said it was annoying but also the one thing he would never want us to change in parenting Aster, because those songs ingrained truths in his mind that will always be there.

We've been intentional about helping Aster get to know the person of Jesus Christ more than lots of Bible characters and stories. As much as we can, we talk with her about Jesus's growing-up years and His life on earth: how He interacts with people, shows kindness, shares with others, loves children, is really patient, and loves to have fun.

Based on what our boys shared with us, we waited longer for her to know Jesus died on a cross, and we haven't gone into detail at all. She doesn't yet understand the "why" behind His sacrifice. We are waiting to have conversations about His death and resurrection, salvation, sanctification, obedience, and the power of the Holy Spirit to change her from the inside out until she can psychologically understand. Our journey with her is also different because her disabilities make abstract concepts extremely difficult for her to understand and actually tend to frustrate her.

There Isn't One Right Way

When Aster was nine, J.J. was driving her to school one morning and noticed she was doodling on some paper she'd found in his truck. After he dropped her off and got to his office, he picked up the pieces of paper and noticed she had written a note that simply said, "I love Jesus."

Aster never talks about God or Jesus unless we bring Him up. She's just not much of a talker. But that day God gave us a glimpse into her heart. It felt like a whisper of hope telling us He was pursuing her, and in time she would come to know and understand His love for her.

There isn't a right way or wrong way to lead our children to Jesus. My story is probably different from yours. I believe God is gracious and that He holds our children accountable for the level of understanding they have at their age. If anything were to happen, I believe Aster would be with Him in heaven. Because, as much as it depends on us and as much as it depends on her, she knows about and loves Jesus.

Jesus, I pray You would draw my children to Your heart and give me courage to trust You with their story and their faith journey. I want to do all I can to tell my children about You and Your love, hoping they will want to follow You. I put so much pressure on myself to get it right. Help me lay down the measuring stick of success versus failure and focus on simply being faithful. Remind me that You simply want me to do the best I can—even if admitting I was wrong with a sincere apology and frozen pizza for dinner is the best I have to offer some days. Amen.

Part Three

What Your Heart
Needs to Know

twenty-one

You Don't Need to Be Perfect

The after-school chaos of homework and my what's-for-dinner rush hour had gotten the best of me. I was also tired of family portraits my kids drew at school where I was either on the computer or the phone. So I came up with some new afterschool rules that would help me get face-to-face time with my boys and prevent the dinner prep crazies.

But on afternoon number three of implementing the new rules, I broke rule number one, which stated I would not talk on the phone until after the boys had snacks and completed their homework, and I had dinner started. Of course, I got distracted on the phone and agreed to let Joshua watch his favorite television show before homework, which broke rule number two, "All homework must be completed before screen time." Joshua's favorite show stretched into another, and before I knew it, I had been on the phone for over an hour.

Hurriedly, I hung up the phone and glanced at the clock. "Oh no," I exclaimed. I needed to shower and get ready before we headed to a friend's house for dinner, and I only had thirty minutes. I shouted downstairs for Joshua to finish his homework.

Forty minutes later, I rushed downstairs in a hurry and noticed Joshua playing in our living room while his *almost* finished homework was strewn across the table with scissors and magazines. I was not a happy mama! My tone was not gentle, and my words gave no indication that love is patient. I ranted about his not cleaning up his mess and threatened to never let him watch TV after school again as we scrambled out the door and jumped in the car.

> I was not a happy mama! My tone was not gentle, and my words gave no indication that love is patient.

Saying I'm Sorry

I could tell Joshua had shut down by his silent stare out the window. "I am sorry I lost my temper with you," I told him. "It bothered me you didn't finish all your homework like you promised. And who should have to clean up your mess on the table?" I asked.

"I should," he answered.

Then the Lord reminded me that I had not carried through on my own promise: to stay off the phone in the afternoons. My hurried, short-fused attitude was my fault. I told Joshua I was wrong for talking to him the way I did and asked, "How did that make you feel?"

His reply: "Like you expect me to be perfect."

"I don't expect you to be perfect, but I do want you to be responsible. Still, I shouldn't have talked to you the way I did. I got on the phone and stayed on it too long, then I realized we were going to be late, and I took it out on you. Will you forgive me?" I asked.

"I forgive you," he said. Then he looked at me and asked, "Mom, how do you expect me to learn to use kind words when you don't even use them with me?"

OUCH! That was a really good question and a painful observation.

I slowed the car, gently reached over to touch his chin, and turned his face toward me. "Can I try again?" I asked.

I repeated almost verbatim what I had said at home. But this time my words were carried by a gentle tone and tucked between pleases and thank-yous. I gave the same warnings but not with the same wrath. The outcome was much more effective.

Jesus tells us in Luke 6:45, "A good man brings good things out of the good stored up in his heart. . . . For the mouth speaks what the heart is full of." Even though God's Spirit in me promises to bring forth the fruit of patience, that day my choices and poor planning allowed anxiety and frustration to choke it out. I let the needs of a friend's phone call come first. That day wasn't what I wanted it to be, but no one could have made it different except me. I chose how I spent my time, and it wasn't my best choice. That choice led me into a tailspin of anxiety and hurry that spilled out of my heart into harsh tones and unkind words to my son.

Being a parent can be incredibly hard, humbling, and refining! God never fails to use my kids to teach me what I want them to learn. Joshua spoke the truth with kind words and honest questions. It was clear he was learning faster than I was.

As hard as it was to hear Joshua call me out, albeit in a very calm and respectful way, I was grateful he did. It gave me the chance to see how I was contradicting the very things we were learning as a family about using kind words and the chance to admit I'd messed up. It also taught me that doing the right thing by apologizing was more important than always doing things right.

The Power of Apology

I never heard my parents apologize, not to each other, not to us, not to anyone. Unfortunately, resentment and unforgiveness were a common denominator in my family. My dad and his brother got into an argument in their late twenties and never spoke to each other again. Both died in their seventies having never reconciled. I have four brothers, and I saw the same pattern of unforgiveness and resentment between them growing up and into adulthood. When I had children, I was determined to do everything I could to stop that precedent. I prayed God would show me how to facilitate healthy conflict resolution and, in my heart, I knew it had to be modeled. But, like most parents, I was hesitant to admit when I messed up and apologize, because I didn't want my children to lose respect or question my credibility as a parent. I took a chance and did it anyway, and the opposite has happened. Whenever I say I am sorry and ask for forgiveness if I've messed up, my kids respect me more, not less.

Tapping into the power of apology has helped create a pattern of reconciliation that strengthened not only our parent-child relationships but also spread into their sibling relationships. Recently, we found out it didn't stop there. When Andrew and Hannah Rose got engaged, J.J. and I did premarital counseling with them. The week we covered communication and dealing with conflict, Hannah Rose said she had never experienced someone saying, "I am sorry. Will you forgive me?" until she met Andrew. She said it helped her see how to work through conflict in a healthy way. Brandi, Joshua's wife, told us something similar in a separate conversation. It made me really glad we were intentional about this, and it made me want to share this part of our story with you.

> Our kids need to hear, see, and experience the power of apology and the healing of forgiveness— in both giving and receiving it.

You and I will never be perfect, and that is a good thing. Our kids can't live up to perfect, and they need to hear us admit we are imperfect. They need to hear, see, and experience the power of apology and the healing of forgiveness—in both giving and receiving it. They need to see humility modeled in our hearts and our home as we own our mistakes and confess our sin. That way they can see how much we need God's grace and forgiveness and realize how much they need it too.

Lord, thank You for showing me I don't have to be perfect. Help me remember that doing the right thing (apologizing) is more important than always doing things right. Give me confidence to be humble and admit when I mess up and ask for my child's forgiveness. I pray our home would be filled with the humility of admission, the kindness of an apology, and the forgiveness of Christ as we seek to make things right with each other and You. Amen.

twenty-two

God Is Doing More
Than You Can See

C ome on, Mom, it's not that bad. Watch meeeee." Those
were Joshua's last words to me before he demonstrated
how easy it was for his nimble eleven-year-old body to
glide down the snow-covered death trap.

We were at an elevation of 8,200 feet in Vail, Colorado, a place
I had dreamed of visiting my whole life, and all I could see was the
danger in front of me. I had been invited to speak at a Christmas
event in Vail, and they'd offered a free four-person pass for skis and
lift tickets if my family wanted to come with me. So, we decided
to cash in all our airline points and take a once-in-a-lifetime trip.

Now I stood at the top of the Rocky Mountains while Joshua
begged me to ski down to meet him. We had gotten off the ski lift together at an intermediate slope, which is what I normally skied back
home. Unfortunately, I hadn't known intermediate slopes in the
Rockies were more difficult than advanced slopes in North Carolina.

Looking down the 60-degree white-powdered incline, I thought, *Surely there is a way to get to the bottom of this steep mountain without risking my life.* But one person after another skied right by me and headed downhill. Not even one glanced my direction, and I knew I was doomed.

I took a deep breath and pushed off, hoping to at least make it to Joshua at the midway point. Surprisingly, I did well—until I swerved off course and hit a huge snowdrift. My skis flew up in the air and so did I, before landing on my back buried under a weighty blanket of snow with my legs twisted like a soft pretzel.

My embarrassment equaled my fear of how much damage I had done to myself and others in the wake of my crash! *That's it!* I thought. *I'm done! These slopes are too steep and there's no way I'm trying that again!*

With the wind knocked out of me, I lay there trying to breathe and assess whether I had broken any bones, while also trying to figure out how to tell Joshua I was quitting, since we had planned to ski together all day. I dug through the snow on my hands and knees, searching for my poles and the ski that had popped off mid-air. Once I had my gear back in place, I got up and slowly made my way to where Joshua waited for me with a half concerned, half trying-not-to-laugh grin on his face.

I was silently rehearsing how I would break the news to him when my thoughts were interrupted by a God-whisper: *Renee, you'll never see or experience all I have for you if you let fear talk you out of it. And you will miss the whole day with your family, skiing in this once-in-a-lifetime place, if you're not willing to take another risk.*

I decided to wait to say anything until we'd made our way to the bottom of the slope together, and by the time we found J.J. and Andrew, thankfully God had talked me out of letting fear get in my way. We found another ski lift together, one that led to slopes much better suited to our experience levels.

That afternoon we ended up on top of a mountain that looked out over miles of snow-capped glory. Sun glistened on the peaks of towering, gray, jagged-edged mountains that stretched across a horizon of deep blue sky. It was the most beautiful sight I had ever seen! I stood there convinced I must be looking at a glimpse of heaven, incredibly grateful and aware that fear had almost kept me from receiving this gift.

When All You See Is Uncertainty

We spent a year conquering a mountain of paperwork and praying mountain-moving prayers as we took our first steps toward adopting a daughter or two from Ethiopia. When it came time to complete our application, we listed our desire to adopt two girls, between four and six years old.

We knew older children were less likely to be adopted, and sibling sets usually waited longer since most families wanted to adopt one child at a time. We also wanted our daughters to have each other to grow up with, the same way our sons had each other, and we didn't want a big age gap between the girls and our boys.

However, when our agency called eleven months later with our adoption referral, God didn't give us two older girls that fit neatly into our family. He gave us the unexpected gift of a severely malnourished six-month-old baby girl who only weighed eight pounds.

Shocked and slightly terrified, I asked our adoption agency how much time we had to decide. They gave us a week. While J.J. was excited, I struggled with feelings of inadequacy and hesitancy. I was forty-two years old and had a very full-time job, plus we had tween-age and teenage sons, both of whom I was desperately trying to figure out how to parent. I also had aging parents with health issues and had absolutely no memory of anything I once knew about babies.

I thought about the risks we would have to take and the uncertainties we would navigate, like medical needs, expenses, and significant changes. I also considered things I'd have to give up, like sleep, convenience, freedom, and familiarity. On top of that, I was concerned Joshua and Andrew might resent us for rearranging their lives forever, and I wondered if our parents and extended family would be supportive.

While I was worrying, God was working. Throughout that week He orchestrated conversations and encouraging situations that were undeniably His confirmation. J.J. reminded me one night that I would never be able to see everything that was ahead, but that God was giving me enough light for the step I was on. And if I was willing to take a step forward in faith, He would then give me enough light for the next step.

> **While I was worrying, God was working.**

As I trusted God more than I listened to my fears, hope started to replace my "need to know" all the details. What I did know, without a doubt, was that God had handpicked Aster to be ours—and that was enough.

Seeing God's Hand, Trusting God's Heart

Looking back over the years, I see a love letter written to our little girl from her heavenly Father on every page of her adoption story. And even in the hardest seasons since Aster came home—months of feeling like I was living in the middle of impossible—I see again and again how God was doing so much more than I realized.

I see God working the unfamiliar things together for good. I see how Aster's infancy, dependency, and special needs forged in us a deeper dependence on God and each other, and created a family bond that pulled our boys closer to us at an age when children typically pull away.

I see God working the overwhelming things together for good. I see how a year of sleepless nights, when Aster was four, brought out servants' hearts in our teenage sons. When Joshua and Andrew saw us struggling with depression caused by sleep-deprivation, they offered to take turns sleeping on a mattress in their sister's room to relieve her anxiety and give us a chance to sleep.

I see God working even the embarrassing things together for good. Like the day a stranger tapped on my car window to see if I was okay because I was crying tears of exhaustion in the parking lot of Aster's speech therapy office. Later that afternoon, I ran out of gas on our way to get Andrew at basketball, after taking Joshua to the doctor for a broken foot, and he had to push my car off the road while wearing his new cast. I see awesome stories for my kids to tell their own children one day.

And on those days when reality doesn't look or feel "good" to me, I ask God to help me see how He is keeping His promise "that in all things God works for the good of those who love him, who have been called according to his purpose" (Rom. 8:28).

Someone Else's Good

What I've discovered is this: God is always working things together for good, *but not just for our good*. Sometimes we are part of His working things together for someone else's good.

You see, I believe Jesus heard a mother in Ethiopia praying for her baby who was starving to death. A mother who was living in the middle of fear and uncertainty unlike anything I've ever known. A mother who knew she could not give her little girl the nurture and nutrition she needed. When God heard that mama's prayers, He tapped on the hearts of a family in North Carolina who loved Him and were called according to His purpose. A family who had been praying about adoption for three years.

God led that praying mom to an orphanage in Ethiopia, who then started searching for a forever family to provide unconditional love and medical care for her severely malnourished baby who had pneumonia. At the same time, God went back to the family in

North Carolina who had been asking Jesus to reveal Himself to them and through them, knowing this baby girl was His answer to their prayers.

And all along, God was working things together to answer a mother's prayers, meet a baby's needs, and fulfill a family's longing to share His love and theirs with another child. He knew we needed the gift of a little girl to light up our world and to remind us each day that He indeed works *all things* together for good!

Don't Let Fear Block Your View

Fear almost kept me from seeing how God wanted to reveal the beauty of His creation and His behind-the-scenes work in our lives, as well as the certainty of His power and presence in the midst of our uncertainties. Not only did fear threaten to block my view, but it also almost kept my kids from experiencing the immeasurable ways God has shown up and shown us His heart through it all.

There will be a million little ways God will work things together for the good of your children, and for your good too, but you may not know it or see it at the time. There will be days when you feel inadequate, uncertain, afraid, and even abandoned. But you will never be alone, no matter what you are facing. Because God is with you, and He is always doing more than you can see.

> There will be a million little ways God will work things together for the good of your children, and for your good too, but you may not know it or see it at the time.

Lord, some days all I can see is uncertainty, and my fear of the unknown threatens to block my view of what You are doing in my life and in my children's hearts. Thank You for reminding me that You are working all things together for good for those who love You and are called according to Your purpose. Even when I can't see how, remind me every day that You are doing more than I can see. Amen.

twenty-three

You Can Do Hard Things

By the time Aster was eight years old, she had been diagnosed with several developmental disabilities. Our biggest concerns were her speech delays, severe social anxiety, multiple learning disabilities, and significant delays in her adaptive life skills. One specialist believed her struggles were attachment related, while another specialist believed the cause was early severe malnourishment or possibly genetics. Without her birth history, medical records, or biological family's medical history, we had no way of knowing so many things.

The collective weight of sadness and uncertainty was overwhelming and more than I could bear some days. I felt an enormous responsibility and deep desire to make sure Aster would reach her fullest potential. The early years felt like we were racing the clock, because a child's brain develops the cognitive skills they need to think, read, learn, remember, reason, and pay attention all between the ages of two and ten years old.

When God Gives Us More Than We Can Handle

After a year of weekly speech and occupational therapy sessions, plus mini sessions at home three times a day, Aster's speech and OT assessments showed only slight improvements in most areas and regression in her memory and processing scores.

Her therapy team explained that any time a child regresses is a red flag, so they wanted Aster to see a pediatric neurologist to rule out silent seizures. I remember feeling the strangest combination of concern, calm, panic, and peace as I listened. But when I got in my car to go home from that visit, I couldn't feel anything except tears rolling down my cheeks.

A week later, J.J. and I met with Aster's IEP team at her school. Peace and strength didn't show up this time, and my tears didn't wait for the car ride home. As we listened to the school psychologist review the results of eight assessments our brave girl had taken, my heart sank. Aster's results were inconsistent, meaning some assessment scores were higher than they had expected compared to many others that were extremely low. The huge variations made it hard for them to determine what category she fell under, which was their goal and an important part of her IEP.

It felt like I had a thousand puzzle pieces but no box top to show me how to put them together.

For the first time in my life, I wanted someone to find a "box" for my child to fit in so I could give her what she needed. I was tired of all the different possibilities and struggles that may or may not be related. It felt like I had a thousand puzzle pieces but no box top to show me how to put them together. I wasn't sure I even had all the pieces, or if I ever would.

I walked out of that meeting with a stack of papers and information I didn't know how to process. And when I got home, I let the weight of it all sink with me into the cushions of my favorite chair. I was too tired to pray, cry, or read my Bible. God had definitely given me more than I could handle.

How Am I Supposed to Do This?

No one could tell us everything we needed to know, and the more I researched, the more overwhelmed I felt. Learning how to parent a child with special needs while navigating hard things our boys were going through and caring for aging parents with health problems, I wondered, *How am I supposed to do this?*

When God called Joshua to step into Moses's leadership shoes and lead the nation of Israel (the whole unbelieving and grumbling lot of them) into the promised land, I imagine Joshua asked the same question.

God had commissioned Joshua with a huge assignment that was more than he could handle. But God didn't just leave Joshua there to figure it out on his own. *God had prepared Joshua* through decades of serving beside and learning from Moses. *God had positioned Joshua* to see the struggles and victories, the blessings and battles of a godly leader, as well as His favor and faithfulness to a person who was fully surrendered to God's calling. *God had promised Joshua* He would be with him and that He would fulfill His plans and give them this land.

God told Joshua to be strong and courageous, and then He told him how:

Be strong and courageous, because you will lead these people to inherit the land I swore to their ancestors to give them. Be strong and very courageous. Be careful to obey all the law my servant Moses gave you; do not turn from it to the right or to the left, that you may be successful wherever you go. Keep this Book of the Law always on your lips; meditate on it day and night, so that you may be careful to do everything written in it. Then you will be

prosperous and successful. Have I not commanded you? Be strong
and courageous. Do not be afraid; do not be discouraged, for the
LORD your God will be with you wherever you go. (Josh. 1:6–9)

Like Joshua's, my assignment was to stay dependent on God's
presence and obedient to His directions. I needed to focus on what
I did know and "refuse to get all tangled up and held back by what
I didn't know. Being present in each day, with a heart bent toward
love and daring to look at what was right in front of me would
be the best place to start."[1]

My responsibility was to respond to God's ability. His Word
promises that He is able to do immeasurably more than I could
think of or imagine, according to His power that is at work within
me and within our family (Eph. 3:20). God knew what Aster, our
boys, and my parents needed. He alone is the only One who is
all-knowing, all-powerful, ever-present, and altogether good (Ps.
147:5; Jer. 10:12–13; Ps. 139:7–12; 31:19–20). I would need to trust
Him more.

As I let go of my need to know everything, God reminded me of
what I did know and what skills I had developed when faced with
harder-than-I-can-handle situations in the past. He encouraged
me to think back on life and work experiences that had prepared
me for this, and to use my project management and strategy skills
to bring my strengths into my circumstances.

One small thing that made a big difference was blocking out
time to sort and split up all the paperwork, and then creating
different three-ring binders to hold research documents, medical
papers, information sheets, treatment possibilities, and treatment
plans for each disability.

God also showed me I was overwhelmed because I was spending
so much time taking care of my little girl that I wasn't giving Him
time to take care of me. He assured me He would provide what
Aster needed if I would be courageous enough to trust Him and
cut back for six months on all the therapy I was doing with her.

Lean on Me

Remember that day our family was skiing in Vail? That afternoon we ended up on another slope that was once again more challenging than we'd expected. Andrew, who was eight years old at the time, was just learning to ski and, bless his heart, he kept falling and getting hurt.

Unfortunately, there was no way down the mountain without skiing. And since I had more experience, I knew the only thing I could do was "ski" Andrew down. I had him stand in front of me with his skis between mine. Then I asked him to wrap his arms around my elbows and hold on tightly and not let go as I guided us down.

It was the craziest thing I'd ever done. And I'm pretty sure we almost died more than once! I remember screaming, "Jesus, help us!" as we slid around sharp curves and down steep inclines. And thankfully, He did! When we finally got to the bottom of the mountain, I told Andrew I was proud of him for keeping his skis straight, staying focused, and trusting me so we could make it down. Much to my surprise, Andrew looked at me and said, "Mom, you did all the work. I just had to lean on you."

We will face hard situations we don't know how to get through and circumstances we wish we could get out of. In those times, God wants us to trust Him instead of trusting our feelings, fears, or frustrations. He invites us to "Trust in the LORD with all [our hearts] and lean not on [our] own understanding; in all [our] ways submit to him, and he will make [our] paths straight (Prov. 3:5–6).

Although I didn't know what Aster's future held, I knew who held her: in her past, her present, and her future.

He knows when we lean on Him, He can guide our decisions and give us direction. That night after our three-hour IEP meeting,

I lay in my favorite chaise lounge and asked God to help me lean on Him the way Andrew had leaned on me. Like strong arms holding me close, God assured me He was with me and would guide me. Although I didn't know what Aster's future held, I knew who held her: in her past, her present, and her future.

Trust in the Lord with All Your Heart

God has called and commissioned you to be your children's mom! But you don't have to figure it all out on your own; God is inviting you to serve beside Him and learn from Him. And on those days when your God-sized assignment as a mom feels like the hardest holy thing you will ever do, remember the same promises, power, and resources God gave Joshua are all available to you!

I know it may not feel like it some days, but God has prepared you for the struggles you face. "Be strong and courageous. Do not be afraid; do not be discouraged, for the LORD your God will be with you wherever you go" (Josh. 1:9). When life gets hard and circumstances feel like more than you can handle, make a list of life experiences and skills you have and ask the Lord to help you think of ways you can use them with your children.

I'm cheering you on, praying you forward, and believing for you, mama! You are loved and held by a strong, good, loving God who promises that *you can do all the hard things through Christ who gives you strength* (Phil. 4:13). His presence is with you, His promises are for you, and His power is in you.

Lord, thank You for Your promise to be with me and to fulfill Your plans for me and my children. You are a good Father I can lean on and trust with all my heart. Help me to stop relying on my own understanding and lean on You instead, knowing that You can make my path straight. When life is

156

hard and I feel inadequate, help me claim Your strength in my weakness and Your triumph in my tears. Now to You who are able to do immeasurably more than all we can think of or imagine, according to Your power that is at work within us, to You be the glory. Amen.

twenty-four

God's Boundaries
Are a Good Thing

{eucalyptus sprig ornament}

I'm not a natural rule-follower or a limit-liker. I love last-minute plans and just-because adventures. If you let me stay up as late as I want and sleep in as long as I can, I will be a very happy girl.

God gave me a soul that craves freedom and a heart that thrives on spontaneity. And that's a good thing—until it's not.

Although I have learned to embrace them, budgets and boundaries are not my friends. When someone tells me I can't do something, I feel a slight suffocation and automatically want to change their mind. In fact, when I hear the phrase "you can't," whether it's said to me or someone else, I instantly feel sad, because to me that usually means freedom, creativity, and fun are off-limits. But once I can see the good between the guardrails, I'm all in!

When J.J. decided it was time to put child locks on our kitchen drawers and cabinets because Aster was getting tall enough to reach inside them. He thought I would be grateful. But instead,

158

when I walked into the kitchen and saw what he was doing, my initial reaction was that I wanted him to take all those newly installed locks right back off.

You see, as I watched J.J. drill little screws into the wood to secure the white plastic child locks, all I could think about was the joy I had seen in Aster's eyes that week when she discovered she could open the drawer that held all the colorful pens and paper clips.

Yet I knew the locks were for her own good. Paper clips aren't safe for a toddler to play with, and other drawers that held more dangerous objects like scissors and matches needed to be off-limits too. It was love that motivated her daddy to put boundaries in place to protect her.

Finding Good between the Guardrails

Have you ever sensed God setting a boundary to protect you, or nudging you to set a boundary you didn't like? There have been countless times I knew God was leading me to set new and needed boundaries (that I initially resisted). It's hard when a boundary feels like a loss or limit of something we tend to want more of. Boundaries can also bring the risk of letting people down or missing out on something we enjoy in the moment.

For instance, when we become moms, our whole lives change and our schedules need to as well. Although we love our babies, losing our free time can be a serious struggle. And, on top of that, we lose the precious commodity of sleep, and our bodies need more of it.

> It's hard when a boundary feels like a loss or limit of something we tend to want more of.

For me, sleep and free time were constantly competing. Once each of my kids started sleeping through the night, I wanted all the freedom I could get in the evenings and during their nap times. I didn't want to go to bed early (I'm a night owl) or take an afternoon nap. But that meant I was exhausted all the time and very grouchy.

As I prayed through the boundaries I sensed God nudging me to set and wrestled with my resistance to needing more rest, I decided to do a word study on *rest* in the Bible. Did you know *rest* is mentioned over one hundred times in Scripture? I didn't know that at the time. I was surprised rest was such a big deal to God. I also discovered rest is a gift from the Lord, and one He desires to give us (Exod. 33:14; Ps. 62:5; 91:1–2; Jer. 6:16; Matt. 11:28–29).

Putting up guardrails on my free time so I could get more rest did not feel like a gift. I wanted the supernatural ability to not need as much sleep. But that's not what God was giving me, so I had to choose my way or His. I could hold tight to what looked and felt like freedom and be a grouchy zombie all week, or I could trust Him and set a boundary on how late I stayed up and rest when my body needed to during the day.

I didn't do it perfectly, but I decided to try my best to get a good night's sleep and supplement with rest during naptime when I needed to. Over time, I could see the gains instead of just losses and feel the good between my new guardrails.

True Freedom

In Psalm 119, King David describes his love for God's boundaries and how they put his heart in the best place to know his Maker and experience the fullness God had for him.

Two of my favorite verses within this psalm are "I run in the path of your commands, for you have broadened my understanding" (v. 32) and "I will walk about in freedom, for I have sought out your precepts" (v. 45). Reading these Scriptures reminds me that when God calls me to live within boundary lines, it's His way of showing me where it is safe for my heart to go.

A few years ago, I started struggling with sadness and discouragement that would come out of nowhere on a daily basis. I didn't know what was causing these feelings, so I decided to pay attention to when they started and what I was doing right before the sadness came.

When I traced my steps to figure out what was going on, social media seemed to be a consistent trigger. But I didn't want social media to be the problem. It kept me company while I was working from home alone or waiting for an appointment, and it gave me something to do while standing in a long checkout line. So, I continued scrolling through my favorite social apps at random times throughout my day.

And the more time I spent in the land of "what everyone else is doing," the more I felt like I wasn't doing enough—not as a mom, wife, friend, or human being. *I should be doing more at home, in our community, in ministry, and online*, I would think.

What I needed to do was set healthy boundaries and daily limits on my social media scroll. I had to get honest with myself and decide if I was going to keep doing something that seemed harmless and felt enjoyable in the moment but left a residue of sadness on my soul. It isn't that social media is bad; it's just that too much of it, too often, is not good for me.

I decided to take a rest from social media for a week to break my habit, and then I set daily and weekly time limits in my phone settings to help me. And once I got over my default habit of picking up my phone for a quick scroll, I started to feel a huge difference emotionally and mentally. I also found a sweet sense of contentment in my everyday life that I had been missing.

> I had to get honest with myself and decide if I was going to keep doing something that seemed harmless and felt enjoyable in the moment but left a residue of sadness on my soul.

Are there boundaries you sense God nudging you to set? Are there areas where you may need to do less of what you want to right now to get what you desire in the long run? What would it look like to set incremental boundaries to move in the direction that reflects the life you long for?

Trusting His Protection

Looking back, I remember feeling like those cabinet locks took freedom away from Aster, but the new limits her daddy put in place actually made it safe for her to roam around the kitchen freely, without the risk of getting hurt. Her daddy could see things she couldn't, and his desire was to protect his daughter from harm. The same is true for us.

Sometimes God will lead us to set a boundary for a season and other times for good. Whether it's overconsuming social media, bingeing on Netflix, doing too much online shopping, not getting enough sleep, eating too much junk food, or other areas in which we sense Him leading us to set boundaries, one thing we can trust is that God's boundaries are His protection and always *for our good.*

Lord, I usually don't like the boundaries I sense I need to set for myself, because they feel like a loss. Please remind me that Your boundaries are always for my good, and Your desire is to set my heart free when I'm willing to walk within the guardrails You create for me. I want to be willing to surrender my time and my life to You so my family can experience the good between Your guardrails in this season of our lives. Help me to number my days with a heart of wisdom and turn away from empty and false illusions of freedom in the things that distract me from what matters most to You and to me. Amen.

twenty-five

What You Do Doesn't Define You

I had been invited by a large Christian radio network based in Charlotte, North Carolina, to do a series of radio interviews to encourage moms. I was so looking forward to it, but the morning of my interview recordings my babysitter canceled. I hated to reschedule, but unless I did, I would have to take four-year-old Aster with me. Not my best option, but I decided to bring her and her best friend, the iPad, with us.

We were all set. She was playing with Dora on her iPad as we pulled into the parking lot ten minutes early. I gathered my things out of the passenger seat, stuck them in my bag, hopped out of the car, pressed the button to unlock the doors, shut my door, and went to get Aster out of her seat.

But her door wouldn't open. I had accidentally locked the doors instead of unlocking them. I panicked a little. Then I reached into my bag to get my keys, but they weren't there! *They have to be here somewhere; my car wouldn't lock if they were still in there,*

I reasoned. I had one of those fancy key fobs with a safety feature for moms like me. It's specially programmed to make your doors automatically unlock if you lock your car with the keys inside.

No keys. I poured my bag out on the gravel parking lot and then looked under my car, and I started to panic again. It was in the middle of August, my car was turned off, my four-year-old daughter was strapped in her car seat inside it, and it was a hundred degrees outside.

I cupped my hands against the driver's window and leaned my forehead against it to see if my keys were in the ignition. Nope— they were sitting on the front passenger's seat. How did I not see them, and why did my car let me lock it?!

J.J. had the only other set of keys, and his office was an hour away from the radio studio. I was now late for my appointment and recording, which made me feel completely irresponsible. Just as this horrible reality hit me, the radio station program director walked out the door and said, "Hi! How are you?"

"Um, not so good." I explained that I'd just locked Aster in my car.

"Well, do you have AAA?" he asked. I didn't.

"Okay, how's she doing?" He looked inside the back window and said, "She looks like she's doing fine."

She and Dora the Explorer were hanging out, and Aster was unfazed by her setup. Thankfully, she was completely unaware she was locked in the car and her mom couldn't open the door.

I started taking deep breaths, hoping the extra oxygen would help me think straight. And then it dawned on me.

"I know what to do! I know we can call 911, because when Joshua was two years old, I did this and I had to call the fire station. And they came."

"Oh, so you have a history of this?"

I smiled and thought to myself. *Why yes, I do.*

We called 911, and they dispatched my call to the local fire department. The radio station was in a really small rural town just outside of Charlotte, and when that big red fire engine pulled into the parking lot, two of the firefighters on it had the biggest grins on their faces. They were so excited to see the radio station and meet the radio personalities. It was like they were on a field trip to meet local celebrities.

Aster still had no idea what was going on. But when she got out of the car, she was so excited as she pointed her finger and said, "Look, Mommy, it's a fire truck."

Watch What You Think

I wanted to crawl under my car and hide, but I couldn't. I needed to get it together and get inside to record my interviews for the morning show. Did I mention these interviews would be aired over the next few weeks because they were hosting an online study for listeners to read through my book *A Confident Heart*? Confidence was the last thing I had to offer that day.

I felt like I was in a daze, trying to gather my thoughts and settle my nerves. I walked through the motions of getting Aster set up in their conference room so she'd be occupied while I recorded. Then I went to the bathroom to freshen up.

Once I was alone, I felt like I'd been cornered by a bully on the playground. *They must think I'm a horrible mom or just stupid—what's wrong with me? Who locks their child in a car on a hot August day? Obviously, it wasn't the first time. Why? Why can't I just get it together?*

And then I thought, *Lord, I'm just not cut out for this. Obviously, I can't manage being a professional and being a mom!*

I'd been in this place before, and I knew it wouldn't end well. Once I recognized what I was saying to myself, I knew I needed to reroute my thoughts.

What you think determines how you feel, and how you feel determines what you say to yourself—and it's usually not very nice.

165

There will be times when it feels like you have failed as a mom, but that does not mean you are a failure as a mom. What you do does not define you.

Tell Yourself the Truth

There are days when discouragement and embarrassment come in for the kill. As a mom, I often let them stay a while and convince me I am unable to do anything right. Too many days in a pit of discouragement have taught me to recognize how easy it is for failure to devour me with feelings of inadequacy and shame.

Thankfully, many of those days have also been filled with hours poring over God's promises and gathering wisdom to help me learn from my mistakes. One thing I learned is that I have an enemy hell-bent on making me believe that *when my best isn't good enough, I'm not good enough.* But God's Word has taught me how to be aware of the devil's schemes and ready to stand against them. In his first letter, Peter tells us how:

> Keep your mind clear, and be alert. Your opponent the devil is prowling around like a roaring lion as he looks for someone to devour. Be firm in the faith and resist him. (1 Pet. 5:8–9 GW)

One of those early discouraging days, after letting my thoughts run wild for a little bit, I knew I needed to get my mind clear. So, I asked the Holy Spirit to help me declutter my thoughts and emotions with the clarity of His truths.

I made a list of *logistical truths* that included facts about what happened: what I did right, what I did wrong, and what I forgot to do at all.

I made a list of *spiritual truths*. Going through my Bible, I found and wrote promises in my journal to remind me of these truths. For example,

> My flesh and my heart may fail,
>   but God is the strength of my heart
>   and my portion forever. (Ps. 73:26)

> The LORD will accomplish what concerns me;
>   Your faithfulness, LORD, is everlasting;
>   Do not abandon the works of Your hands.
>   (Ps. 138:8 NASB)

You + God = Enough

I also made a list of *circumstantial truths* about my reality at that time that made my circumstances really hard: a close friend died, we adopted a baby from Ethiopia, our boys changed schools, my mom was hospitalized and moved in with us afterward, my father had to have emergency quadruple bypass heart surgery, and I had to have two biopsies after an abnormal mammogram—all within six months' time.

I was exhausted, overwhelmed, and unable to keep up. But my unrealistic expectations of myself had blinded me from seeing that I needed to give myself more margin and let others know I couldn't balance it all.

In the end, I had to accept that although I had physically done the best I could, it wasn't always enough. *But it didn't mean I wasn't enough.*

> I had to accept that although I had physically done the best I could, it wasn't always enough. *But it didn't mean I wasn't enough.*

On the days your failures make you feel like you are not enough, pause and remember you are not your failures. Tell yourself the truth: you are enough. Sometimes circumstances and challenges don't give you sufficient margin to do your best. So, what do you do? Take time to clear your mind and your schedule so you can make the adjustments you need.

Jesus, help me remember I am not defined by what I do, good or bad. I am defined by the love for me You demonstrated when You died on the cross. Infuse me with self-kindness and a willingness to give myself grace, and give me a chance to grow every single day. Help me develop wisdom to learn from my mistakes and stop labeling myself for them. Remind me with loving conviction that I am a child of God, holy and dearly loved by You, and that is the only label that belongs on me! Amen.

twenty-six

You Don't Have to Do It All

I feel completely numb," she said to me. "I don't want to be a mom or a wife anymore. In fact, I know I could walk out on my family today and not feel anything . . . but it would devastate them. And I can't do that because I care about them. I just don't have anything left in me to give or feel. And I don't know what to do."

I stood there stunned, not knowing what to say. It wasn't what she said that shocked me but the fact that she was the second woman at this conference who had come to me within the past twenty-four hours with such a brave and raw confession.

Two women. Numb and empty. Surviving but not really living.

There are days when I feel overwhelmed and defeated before my feet even hit the floor. The responsibilities of motherhood can be overwhelming. And I know I'm not alone.

That morning at the conference I had shared my own struggles and rock-bottom burnout story. I'd shared how ten years earlier I'd asked God, *Why?* Why after being a Christian for over a decade was I so miserable?

Hadn't Jesus said He came to give us life to the full? I needed to know how and when He was going to keep that promise to me, because the only things that filled my life were obligations, stress, and hurry.

Drained by All the Doing

Kids' activities, church commitments, playdates and Bible studies, family time, service projects, neighborhood ministry, and trying to leave a legacy. These were all good "Christian" things I was doing. I assumed my commitments reflected Christ and hopefully pleased Him.

Surely it's just a phase, I told myself. *Things will slow down, and I'll start enjoying my life eventually.*

But life wasn't slowing down, and I wasn't enjoying anything.

Drained by all the doing, I was numb, exhausted, and depleted. I couldn't keep going. My heart was checking out, and just like these two women, I was scared of the *me* I didn't know anymore.

> My undoing was of my own doing. My doing and doing and doing . . .

I needed to get honest with myself and God about where I was and how I got there.

And when I started asking hard questions and listening to my heart and His, He showed me something I needed to see.

My undoing was of my own doing. My doing and doing and doing . . .

Surrender

Standing there, I sensed this overwhelmed mom was holding her breath, waiting to see what I would say now that she'd spilled her guts. I looked into her eyes and told her, "I understand. I've been there."

170

I told her how I'd come to the end of my own rope. Over time, I had started doing and serving more and more—while seeking God less and less. Yet in my mixed-up understanding, I assumed serving God was the same as seeking Him. I thought extreme busyness was the Christian norm: the life God wanted for me, the life God expected of me. But I was wrong.

I didn't want to tell anyone I wasn't up for the task because they all seemed to be handling their crazy-busy lives fine. It was just me who couldn't keep up.

Here's the best word I had for her, and for you: *surrender*. Surrender your time to God; surrender your motivation, your emotions, and even your numbness. For me, surrendering happens when I empty my thoughts and heart of all that I'm carrying and let go of everything I want or think needs to happen. Each week I try to take time to sit with my calendar open, and I ask God to help me plan. I ask Him to show me His priorities for my days.

> Surrendering happens when I empty my thoughts and heart of all that I'm carrying and let go of everything I want or think needs to happen.

You Don't Have to Do What You've Always Done

One of our biggest challenges as moms is around the holidays. One year not too long ago, I remember closing my eyes and pressing two fingers gently on my right eyelid, hoping that would stop the twitching. My brain would not stop listing all the things I needed to do, gifts I needed to buy, and plans and decisions I needed to make! Then there was laundry to wash, groceries to get, appointments to schedule, calls to return, and Aster's December birthday to plan for.

171

Why can't everything else just do itself in December so I can handle all the extra stuff that comes with Christmas? I thought.

As I walked around my house in what felt like circles, trying to make progress, I felt my chest getting tight. I didn't want to resent December or dread Christmas, and I was the only person who could stop that from happening. So, I sat down and made a list of my nonstop thoughts, ideas, desires, expectations that I assumed others had of me, and our family's Christmas traditions. I looked at the list and took a deep breath; no wonder I was overwhelmed and eye-twitchy.

Then I told myself something I desperately needed to hear: *You don't have to do it all.*

Of course, I argued back with myself. *How can I not do some of these things? I've always done them!*

Then a new thought came to me: *You don't have to do what you've always done. You could just do what matters most to you—and the ones you love.*

It sounded like something someone older and wiser would say; I knew it was straight from God's heart to mine. And I felt His grace-filled perspective shift something in me. I didn't have to do it all. I was an adult, and I could decide.

Now, I'm sure this would be an obvious option to some people, but it was the first time I'd considered such a radical concept at Christmas. And I knew I liked the idea when it brought a sense of relief in my soul and calm in my chest.

I put up fewer Christmas decorations, bought teachers gift cards instead of gifts, and did all my shopping online. I wrote down the traditions that mattered most to me, and I sat down with J.J. and our kids to find out what mattered most to them.

That Christmas, we didn't do everything we had always done, and I enjoyed it more than I ever had before. I also took J.J.'s advice and gave each family member an activity to plan. That way I wasn't the only one in charge of food, games, and activities. It's a glorious thing when your kids become young adults. (Just hold on, young mamas, your time is coming!)

But you know, it's not only during the holidays that we fall into this mindset. Every season, every stage, has its celebrations, expectations, and preparations that can leave us frazzled and disconnected from what matters most. *Sweet friend, you don't have to do it all.* At Christmas or any other time of year.

The Next Right Thing

"God has said, 'Never will I leave you. . . .' So we say with confidence, 'The Lord is my helper'" (Heb. 13:5–6). When we get overwhelmed, we can ask for God's help to know what to let go of and how to order the tasks on our list. We also need to get better at saying no. It just comes natural for us to be multitaskers and people pleasers. I don't know any woman who doesn't want to be there for everyone she knows, whether at work or church or with friends. And I'm right there too. I don't want to disappoint anybody. For some reason, I feel like I have to be it all and do it all.

But the truth is, we can't be and do it all. What we can do is learn to say no to a lot of requests for our time. That way we'll have the energy and emotion to give to our kids. We are always going to disappoint someone, but we won't be as likely to disappoint those we love most—which includes God and our family. And when I feel completely overwhelmed, I remind myself of something my friend and author Emily Freeman always says: *I'll do the next right thing in love.*

Sometimes the next right thing is to do a load of laundry. Or make a grocery list. Or get ready for work. Whatever it is, just focus on that one thing until it's done. And then move on to your next right thing. If you need to, bow out of some commitments and come up with a load you can live with and love. One that eases all the eye twitches and chest pains, amen!

The Best Right Thing

The apostle Paul writes,

> For this reason I kneel before the Father, from whom every family
> in heaven and on earth derives its name. I pray that out of his glori-
> ous riches he may strengthen you with power through his Spirit in
> your inner being, so that Christ may dwell in your hearts through
> faith. And I pray that you, being rooted and established in love,
> may have power, together with all the Lord's holy people, to grasp
> how wide and long and high and deep is the love of Christ, and to
> know this love that surpasses knowledge—that you may be filled
> to the measure of all the fullness of God. (Eph. 3:14–19)

My friend Andrea shared with me how this passage hit her one
day as she read it: Paul is on his knees praying for Christ to dwell
within the Christians in Ephesus *so that* they understand how
much God loves them. Not so that they can go do more, preach
more, or achieve more. The highest call, and the desire of Paul's
prayers, is that we grasp the fullness of God's love for us. Period.

*Lord, there are days when I am absolutely drained by all
of the things I do, and I feel like I'll never get everything
done. Help me remember that being overwhelmed is okay
for a season, but living in a constant state of overwhelm is
not healthy nor honoring to You. Teach me how to leave
enough margin in my days for interruptions and unexpected
situations. Please give me the courage to say no when I need
to so I can say yes to the people and commitments that are
most important to You and to me, in this season of being
a mom. Amen.*

twenty-seven

Guilt Is Stealing Time
You Don't Have to Lose

W e recently spent a weekend out of town, helping Andrew and his wife, Hannah Rose, work on some home
renovations that needed to get done so they could
rent their house on Airbnb. They had both started new jobs an
hour away and had already moved into an apartment, but they
hadn't lived in their house long enough to sell it. Since the house
was empty, I decided to stay a few extra days there to have focused
time to work on my book manuscript and to do a few small house
projects in the evenings.

When I got home a few days later, I still had work to finish on
my book, so we decided to pretend I was still out of town. I stayed
upstairs and worked in my home office from dawn to dusk. All
week, guilt seeped into my thoughts with a twisted script telling
me how horrible I was to be writing a book to encourage moms
when I wasn't spending "enough" time with my child.

One night, J.J. was putting Aster to bed, and from my office I could hear them playing with our two dachshunds. We have a tradition every night called "doggy playtime" where our two dogs chase each other and play, and it's just a fun before-bedtime thing. Soon J.J. and Aster would read a book together and say bedtime prayers. I hadn't spent much time with Aster that whole week, but that evening I had to keep working so I could meet a deadline I had already needed to push back.

I longed to be with them, laughing and carefree, connecting with my girl. But I also knew I needed to focus on writing. Guilt had also been bullying me for extending my deadline, telling me how irresponsible I was for not being done even though my delay was caused by migraines and severe back pain I couldn't control.

Let Love Lead

That night, I was determined to ban guilt from driving my decisions. Instead, I wanted to let love lead. I wanted to walk away from work for a little while, and I wanted to be with my family. Compelled by love and not guilt, that's just what I did.

But before I walked out of my office, I decided guilt had already taken enough of my time. Mommy-guilt was not getting any of the ten minutes I had to be with Aster and J.J. Instead, I would walk into the room and not mention that I felt bad.

Unless Aster's body language or her words told me she was upset with me, I wasn't going to waste one minute on the guilt script in my head that read like this: *I'm so sorry I haven't spent time with you. I've really wanted to, and I feel so bad about it.*

I was not going to secretly hope my daughter would say something to make me feel less guilty. I wanted to focus on Aster and be fully present with her, to give her my undivided attention, hugs, laughter, and love during all six hundred seconds we had together.

When guilt came for me that night, it tried to steal my focus and take time I didn't have to lose. In the past, I had gone along with it. But fortunately, this time I recognized what was happening and interrupted my thoughts. I said to myself, *Nope. I am not going to focus on the big chunks of time I cannot give. Instead, I am going to offer the little that I have. I'm going to stop what I'm doing that is stirring up mom-guilt (working long hours and at night), so I can give my child and myself the gift of time together.*

Mom-guilt tries to convince us that we are not doing enough and that our children think we're the worst! When I got into Aster's room and told her I wanted to be part of doggy playtime, she didn't mention that she missed me. She didn't ask why I hadn't spent more time with her. She had not been thinking, *Where's my mom? I can't believe she isn't spending time with me. She's such a bad mom! Other moms would be spending time with their children.*

> Mom-guilt tries to convince us that we are not doing enough and that our children think we're the worst!

Guilt is a thief that steals from the past and the present. It steals our time, our energy, and our focus by getting us to think about all we are not doing or "should" be doing when we could just *do* the thing. Spend the time. Make the call. Say the apology. Send the text. Leave the sticky note.

I didn't have two hours to spend with Aster that night, but I did have ten minutes. And I knew God would multiply my time if I was willing to take a step of faith and step away from my desk and a deadline that demanded my attention.

Our kids are willing to give us a lot more grace than we realize. We just need to step into that grace and be what we can be. We don't have time to lose, and we don't have to lose the time we have by giving in to guilt. Let's live fully in what we can do while refusing to feel guilty for what we can't do.

Parenting without Regrets

Author and podcaster Laura Tremaine has inspired me with three statements she uses to help her make decisions: *I sometimes regret, I never regret,* and *I always regret.*[1] When I ask myself to finish these statements, they give me clarity and help me make decisions on how I spend my time. I call them my guilt-prevention guides.

I Sometimes Regret

I sometimes regret things I've said to my kids.

I sometimes regret time wasted scrolling on social media.

I sometimes regret telling my child no too quickly.

I sometimes regret saying yes to too many commitments.

I sometimes regret giving other people more time than I give my family.

I Never Regret

I never regret reading a book with my child.

I never regret playing a game with my kids.

I never regret calling or texting my adult children.

I never regret giving my children words of encouragement.

I never regret reading my Bible or writing in my journal.

I Always Regret

I always regret being impatient, hurried, and distracted.

I always regret beating myself up with mom-guilt and shame.

I always regret overreacting instead of calmly responding.

I always regret not having enough margin to spend time with my child.

I always regret wishing I could do more instead of just doing what I can.

These lists remove me from the role of prisoner and make me the prison guard of my guilt. They allow me to move from an emotional trap and assess my time through a logical filter.

Guilt Prevention

We know we'll be happier, more positive, more loving moms if we take time for ourselves, but how often do we take time away from our kiddos only to feel guilty the whole time we're gone? There's the guilt we feel when we leave our kids, and there's the guilt we feel when we're grouchy because we haven't been away from our kids.

Instead of feeling guilty for taking time for yourself, start looking at your time away as guilt prevention. It prevents the mom-guilt that comes from being grumpy with your kids because you needed a break but felt too guilty to take it.

> There's the guilt we feel when we leave our kids, and there's the guilt we feel when we're grouchy because we haven't been away from our kids.

If you're like me, and there are times you feel guilty when you've planned a night out with friends, for example, take a minute to assess whether there's a reason or if it's just another mom-guilt script. Sometimes there is a cause. Sometimes I, for example, haven't spent much time with my family that week. I've taken care of them by cooking and doing laundry, but I've been on the phone and computer a lot and haven't had much face-to-face quality time with them.

In those instances, instead of just feeling guilty, let's take that as a cue to intentionally connect with our kids, even if it's just for thirty minutes one night that week. Taking time to plan a date with our family prevents us from feeling guilty when we are out with friends and gives us the gift of quality time with our kids!

Lord, help me to give myself grace when I feel guilty for something I did or didn't do. Instead of wasting my mental and emotional energy thinking about what I should have done, and giving guilt too much time, help me do what I can and make the most of the minutes and moments You have given me with my children. Thank You for grace that cancels all guilt trips, because my guilt was canceled on the cross by Jesus. Amen.

twenty-eight

God Loves You and Wants to Be with You

O ur life was starting to look like an avalanche of un-expected circumstances and unpredictable schedules. Plans had to be changed. Commitments had to be canceled. And there was no end in sight. On top of all that, a constant splay of toys on the floor made me feel like our house was a mess all the time. Add all that together, plus not enough sleep, and my heart started battling anxiety and a not-so-nice-to-be-around attitude.

I decided to list all my racing thoughts and accumulating concerns in my journal and spend time with Jesus praying over them and asking Him to help me. I read Scripture to remind me that we make plans but God ultimately directs our course. And I wrote down promises from Scripture on an index card, knowing that memorizing these was the best way to help my mind focus on trusting God's sovereignty in the midst of our uncertainty.

My time with the Lord was so good, I decided to write a commitment in my journal to spend fifteen minutes (or more) alone with Him each day. Normally, I spend some time with the Lord each day, but when life spirals like it was at that time, the gravitational pull of trying to manage the chaos can knock me off-kilter. I knew writing my commitment down would help me. And for the first few days I was consistent, spending quiet time reading my Bible, praying, and journaling. But by the next Friday I had gone a few days without any time alone with God, and I was running on empty.

Running on Empty

When Jesus met her, she was running an errand and running on empty as she ran away from the rejection of the women in her small town and walked by herself to the well that day at noon. Pursuing her with His perfect love, Jesus timed it so she would run into Him.[1]

You may know her as the Samaritan woman, but I like to call her Sam because it makes her feel more like the real woman she was: a woman just like you and me. A woman who longed to be pursued, known, wanted, and loved.

Jesus knew Sam would be there, so He waited while His disciples went to town to get lunch. He initiated a conversation by asking her to give Him a drink. When He spoke, Sam heard gentleness in His voice and kindness and humility in His request for some water. In His eyes, she saw acceptance and love, not judgment or shame.

She was surprised that He (a Jewish man) was talking to her, but she must have enjoyed His company and their conversation because she didn't hurry to leave. They talked about everything from religion to relationships, from where she should worship to what true worship was. Sam was surprised by how much Jesus knew about her, especially that she'd had five husbands and the man she was currently living with wasn't her husband.

"You must be a prophet," she said. Assuming He was a religious man, she told Jesus, "'I know that Messiah' (called Christ) 'is

God Loves You and Wants to Be with You

coming. When he comes, he will explain everything to us.' Then Jesus declared, 'I, the one speaking to you—I am he'" (John 4:25–26).

Jesus's disciples returned at that moment, and Sam decided to head back home so she could invite the people from her town to meet Jesus. No longer running away in shame, Sam ran toward the people who had hurt her, offering the hope she found in the One who healed her. The time she spent with Jesus gave her self-awareness and spiritual wholeness she didn't want to keep to herself.

This was the Messiah she had waited for. Love had pursued her because He wanted to be *with her*. Their time together that day marked the beginning of a relationship that would change Sam's life forever.

She Stopped and She Stayed

Things would have been so different if Sam had given Jesus a drink and then hurried off to finish her errands and her to-do list, but that's not what happened. Sam stopped and she stayed. She let time unfold into a meaningful conversation, where Jesus spoke words of wisdom and assurance into the depths of her soul. He gave her the spiritual insights, understanding, and conviction her heart needed.

Like Sam, I was running on empty and running from an angst inside of me that I needed to deal with. I needed to slow down and be with Jesus, but my schedule that afternoon told me I had a babysitter coming to take the kids somewhere so I could clean our house without interruptions, and surely *that* would give me the peace I longed for.

After the babysitter came and took the kids to the park, I started picking things up off the floor, straightening the house in preparation for deep cleaning. But my thoughts were interrupted by a quiet voice in my heart: *You could spend some of this quiet time alone with Me.*

I quickly reminded the still small voice that I was paying a baby-sitter $10 an hour. Without skipping a beat, the voice gently asked, *Is your time with Me not worth $10?*

> No matter how hard we try, we can't stay in the peace of God's promises and the wisdom of His Word unless we slow down and spend time with Him.

I felt so convicted and a bit frustrated. Wanting to protest "giving up" time to clean my house so I could enjoy peace with everything in place, I took a few deep breaths and waited to see if that Holy Spirit prodding went away. It didn't.

I knew lightning wasn't going to strike me if I chose to ignore His nudge, but I also knew I would be choosing to ignore Jesus, who was pursuing me because He wanted to spend time with me.

An Illusion of Peace

I could hold on tight to an illusion of peace that would evaporate minutes after my kids got home, or I could be held by the One who holds all things together, including me (Col. 1:17). I could clean my house, or I could let Jesus clean my heart out and show me what was really going on inside. I decided to stop and to stay. I put my to-do list down, knowing time with the Lord was what I needed—and it would be worth a whole lot more than $10!

That afternoon, as I spent quiet time with Jesus, He helped me see that I was grasping for control because our unpredictable schedule and having to cancel some commitments made me feel like a failure. He also assured me that I was living in a season, not a permanent situation. And He reminded me that our house would look like children lived in it for several years, so I needed to decide if I wanted our kids to feel like they were living in a home or a museum.

I wanted a clean house. But a clean house wasn't what I needed that day. A clean house couldn't give me lasting peace, and getting all the toys off the floor wasn't going to provide the wisdom I desperately needed to help me navigate these big adjustments with grace.

Heart and Soul Care

No matter how hard we try, we can't stay in the peace of God's promises and the wisdom of His Word unless we slow down and spend time with Him. Scripture encourages us, "If any of you lacks wisdom, let him ask God, who gives generously to all without reproach, and it will be given him" (James 1:5 ESV). Only God can give us the wisdom we need for daily decisions and the moment-by-moment parenting journey we are on. Through time with Him in Scripture and talking to Him throughout our day, we can stay close to Jesus and ask Him to guide our thoughts, our steps, and our house cleaning schedule.

> He invites you to come to Him to experience what it's like to be loved, not for what you do but simply because you are His.

Here are some simple ways to let God love you, through intentional heart and soul care:

- **Whisper a prayer** before your feet touch the floor each morning. Invite Jesus into your day and ask Him to pour enough of His grace and truth into your heart to give you an abundance of what you need and enough to share with your children. *"Show me your ways, Lord, teach me your paths. Guide me in your truth and teach me, for you are God my Savior, and my hope is in you all day long" (Ps. 25:4-5).*

- **Take time to read God's Word** or listen to Scripture in a Bible app. Ask Jesus to increase your hunger for His Word and for your awareness of His presence. *"For everything that was written in the past was written to teach us, so that through the endurance taught in the Scriptures and the encouragement they provide we might have hope"* (Rom. 15:4).

- **Listen to worship music,** Christian audio books, and podcasts that encourage your heart. *"Faith comes from hearing the message, and the message is heard through the word about Christ"* (Rom. 10:17).

- **Surround yourself** with friends who encourage you in your relationship with God and in your role as a mom. Pray for and encourage them too. *"The sweetness of a friend comes from his earnest counsel"* (Prov. 27:9 ESV).

God pursues you because He wants to be with you, in your ups and in your downs. He wants to encourage and help you as a mom, but more than anything He wants to love and lead you as His child. He invites you to come to Him to experience what it's like to be loved, not for what you do but simply because you are His.

Lord, help me believe the promises of Your love for me. When I feel frustrated, overwhelmed, or invisible, remind me that You see me, and You are pursuing me because You want to be with me and talk to me. You are the only One who can help me see what my heart really needs. I want to value my time with You more and find creative ways to be with You no matter how busy I am. Help me pull away from "the crowds" of life and find a quiet place to let You take care of my heart and soul. Amen.

twenty-nine

You've Got What It Takes to Be a Confident Mom

❧

R eed Gold Mine in North Carolina is the site of the first
documented gold found in the United States, and I had
no idea it was located only forty-five minutes from our
house until a friend told me about it. Once Joshua and Andrew
were old enough, we took a family field trip one Saturday to pan
for gold and learn all about the mine's history.

"The life of farmer John Reed would have been long forgotten
had it not been for a chance event one Sunday in 1799," when his
"son Conrad found a large yellow rock in Little Meadow Creek,"
which was located on the family farm. The "rock reportedly
weighed 17 pounds, and for three years was used as a doorstop
at the Reed house."[1]

In 1802, a jeweler who was passing through the area identified
the gold nugget and purchased it for the asking price of $3.50. Reed
had no idea at the time that it was worth $3,500. The following

year he formed a partnership with three local men and began the Reed mining operation.

While we were at the mine, we went on a tour of one of the original mineshafts. Walking down thirty steps into the cold, damp, and dark cave that tunneled underground, I imagined the miners cramped in that tight space, chipping away at walls of hardened mud and rock every day. They were willing to invest endless hours in the mine because they knew the value of what they might find. I am sure there were days when they felt like their time was wasted as they headed back home without their sought-after treasure. But they returned, ready to dig again, knowing that might be the day they discovered the earth's hidden wealth.

As we were leaving the visitors center, I noticed a small placard with the history of Reed Gold Mine on it. The last sentence stated that John Reed was a wealthy man when he died in 1845. As I read those words, I thought to myself, *John Reed was a wealthy man long before he died. He became a wealthy man the day he acquired that property.* The gold had always been there, but its value wasn't realized until it was brought to the surface. And the same is true for our children. The gold is in there; we just need to help bring it to the surface.

The Next Chapter Is Up to You

Like gold miners, we will need time, awareness, patience, and perseverance to discover and develop the gold of God's character hidden in our children's hearts. Time will be required to notice and nurture our children with encouragement, affirmation, acceptance, and love. Awareness will be necessary to see those nuggets of kind words, sharing, acceptance, responsibility, and more peeking through the dirt. The more aware we are, the more gold we'll see. Patience will be needed as we dig through the dirt and look past our children's flaws to see the treasure of God's image hidden in their hearts. Perseverance will be essential to help us not give up on the hard days, when it feels like we're wasting our time. As we confidently persevere in shaping our children's hearts, we also need to remember God is shaping ours.

On those days when we get frustrated, let's take a deep breath and try to remember how much God loves us, how patiently He leads us, and how lovingly He corrects us. As my friend Emily says, let's remember,

> we have a gift right now in this moment, an opportunity to welcome God's grace and free ourselves from the traps of self-labeled inadequacies.
>
> Now is your chance to tell yourself the truth. You are measuring up, you are doing a good job and you are enough, just as you are. Your story isn't over. Your legacy is yet to be defined. The next chapter is up to you![2]

You Are More Than a Mom

When Andrew was nineteen years old, I was working on a small writing assignment and asked him to help me. All I needed was for him to tell me what makes a mother "more than a mom." Here is what he said: "A mom is the heart of her home. She creates a place where her kids feel like they belong, a place where they always feel accepted, loved, and wanted. A place where they can be goofy and not be judged."

> Your story isn't over. Your legacy is yet to be defined. The next chapter is up to you!

I smiled for days, knowing this was the same son who, six months earlier, had told me he couldn't wait to move out, live on his own, and go to college in a different state almost three hours away.

Whether we are moms of littles or bigs, children who were birthed with our bodies or birthed in our hearts through love and prayers, our worth is beyond measure! Our role is beyond description. And what we do every day matters—so much more than we may ever know!

We are a safe place to come home to. We are a soft place to land when life knocks our kids down. We are the cheerleader they need and the coach they avoid. We are the person they want when they are sick or when they feel lost. We are heart-shapers, memory-makers, purpose-instillers, boundary-setters, prayer-warriors, and dream-encouragers.

As we finish this part of our journey together, here is one last thing I want you to remember: *you* are an overcomer and more than a conqueror. You're a child of the one true King, who delights in you! Jesus is for you, and He is with you. When days get hard, press on, mom, and have hope because God is faithful. He sees beyond who you are today to who you can become. Because you are His and He is yours, you've got everything you need to become a confident mom!

Lord, thank You for seeing me through the lens of a gold miner and for helping me learn how to do the same. I pray You would keep inspiring me and reminding me to carve out time to focus on what matters most: discovering and developing who You created my children to be by noticing and nurturing Your character qualities in them. Help me become more aware, patient, and persevering in the process. I want to become a confident mom in Christ through my dependence on Your love for me. When I doubt that I have what it takes, help me recognize the source of my uncertainty and bring it all to You. I want to acknowledge and rely on You every day, trusting You to help me navigate the hard parts of parenting, holding tight to Your promises, and fighting for the legacy of my family. Amen.

thirty

From My Heart to Yours

As children of God, we were designed to find our identity, our significance, and our confidence in Him. But the only way we'll have lasting soul-confidence and security in Christ is if we move beyond knowing about God to really knowing Him and relying on Him with our heart, mind, and soul.

A personal relationship with God sets us free to be all we were created to be. When we respond to His invitation and accept Jesus's gift of salvation, we don't just accept a new philosophy of life. We establish a personal relationship with our Creator, the One who knows us, loves us, and accepts us and also desires our transformation so we can become all He created us to be.

Maybe, like me for so many years, you have heard about Him or you have even believed in Him, but you haven't really believed Him. At least you don't always feel or live like His promises are true for you. Maybe you know in your head God loves you and the Bible says He forgives you, but you still beat yourself up with condemnation and guilt, even though you may be familiar with

His promise that "there is no condemnation for those who belong to Christ Jesus" (Rom. 8:1 NLT). "For in him all things were created: things in heaven and on earth, visible and invisible . . . all things have been created through him and for him. He is before all things, and in him all things hold together" (Col. 1:16–17).

Today can be the day the gospel of grace moves from your head to your heart, and you really start living in God's truth. Today can be the day you let your desire to be known and loved, just as you are, lead you into a personal and intimate relationship with Jesus.

The first step is to embrace your imperfections in light of God's perfect love, "being confident of this, that he who began a good work in you will carry it on to completion until the day of Christ Jesus" (Phil. 1:6).

I also know it's possible you're in a different place. A new place. An unknown place. Maybe you know about God yet don't know God or have a relationship with Him, but you want to or at least you'd like to know more. I am so glad you are here on this journey with me. I know how much God wants to give you His grace and truth and invite you into a personal relationship through Jesus so you can be set free through His forgiveness and experience the fullness of His love.

Through Jesus's death and resurrection, God offers His mercy and grace, new life through the Holy Spirit, and lasting soul-security through a relationship with Christ. If you would like to accept Jesus as Lord of your life, you can pray the words I've written below or use my prayer as a guide to create your own. Just talk to God from your heart with honesty and sincerity.

Lord, I have done things that have separated me from You and other people. The Bible says You love me so much You sacrificed Your only Son, Jesus, so that anyone who believes in Him will be forgiven and have eternal life. Lord, I believe in Him and want to believe His promise to set me free from condemnation for my past, present, and future sins. I could never earn Your grace or salvation by my good works, so I put my trust in what Jesus did for me on the cross. I want You to be Lord of my life. Thank You for loving me, pursuing me, accepting me, and wanting Your best for me now and for eternity. In Jesus's name. Amen.

Sweet friend, wherever you are, Jesus meets you there. Although we are not worthy of His sacrificial love and can never do anything to deserve it, we are worth His love because He chose to give it to us. We are His! Hold on to this promise and live in the power of its truth: because God's love is perfect, you don't have to be!

If you want to know more about a relationship with Jesus or first steps to help you get to know Him and His Word, visit reneeswope .com/more-about-jesus.

193

what God's Word says

30 Promises to Replace Your Doubts with God's Truth

When You Say . . .	God's Word Says
Being a mom is overwhelming.	Trust in the LORD with all your heart; do not depend on your own understanding. Seek his will in all you do, and he will show you which path to take. Proverbs 3:5–6 NLT
I hate who I become when I am angry with my kids.	Be quick to listen, slow to speak and slow to become angry, because human anger does not produce the righteousness that God desires. James 1:19–20
I'm not doing enough.	"My grace is all you need. My power works best in weakness." So now I am glad to boast about my weaknesses, so that the power of Christ can work through me. 2 Corinthians 12:9 NLT
I don't know enough about the Bible.	If you need wisdom, ask our generous God, and he will give it to you. He will not rebuke you for asking. James 1:5 NLT

When You Say . . .	**God's Word Says**
No matter how hard I try, it's never enough.	The humble will see their God at work and be glad. Let all who seek God's help be encouraged. Psalm 69:32 NLT
I'm such a bad mom.	Your statutes are wonderful; therefore I obey them. The unfolding of your words gives light; it gives understanding to the simple. Psalm 119:129–30
I feel overwhelmed by all my options and everyone's opinions.	Show me the right path, O LORD; point out the road for me to follow. Lead me by your truth and teach me, for you are the God who saves me. All day long I put my hope in you. Psalm 25:4–5 NLT
I'm not spending enough time with my kids.	Teach us to number our days carefully so that we may develop wisdom in our hearts. Psalm 90:12 CSB
I don't have what it takes to be a good mom.	For [you] are God's masterpiece. He has created [you] anew in Christ Jesus, so [you] can do the good things he planned for [you] long ago. Ephesians 2:10 NLT
I keep messing up.	Without good direction, people lose their way; the more wise counsel you follow, the better your chances. Proverbs 11:14 MSG
What if my kids don't follow Jesus?	Never stop praying. . . . God's kindness is intended to lead [us] to repentance. 1 Thessalonians 5:17 NLT; Romans 2:4
I wish I knew what God wants me to do.	Imitate God, therefore, in everything you do, because you are his dear children. Live a life filled with love, following the example of Christ. He loved us and offered himself as a sacrifice for us, a pleasing aroma to God. Ephesians 5:1–2 NLT

When You Say . . .	**God's Word Says**
I feel guilty all the time.	[Your] flesh and [your] heart may fail, but God is the strength of [your] heart and [your] portion forever. Psalm 73:26
I don't have enough time to spend with God or read my Bible.	God's laws are perfect. They protect us, make us wise, and give us joy and light. God's laws are pure, eternal, just. They are more desirable than gold. They are sweeter than honey dripping from a honeycomb. For they warn us away from harm and give success to those who obey them. Psalm 19:7–11 TLB
I'm failing at motherhood.	May Jesus himself and God our Father, who reached out in love and surprised you with gifts of unending help and confidence, put a fresh heart in you, invigorate your work, enliven your speech. 2 Thessalonians 2:17 MSG
I have no patience.	May God, who gives this patience and encouragement, help you live in complete harmony with each other, as is fitting for followers of Christ Jesus. Romans 15:5 NLT
My life feels impossible.	Jesus looked at them intently and said, "Humanly speaking, it is impossible. But with God everything is possible." Matthew 19:26 NLT
What if my kids make the same mistakes I made?	Don't fret or worry. Instead of worrying, pray. Let petitions and praises shape your worries into prayers, letting God know your concerns. Before you know it, a sense of God's wholeness, everything coming together for good, will come and settle you down. It's wonderful what happens when Christ displaces worry at the center of your life. Philippians 4:6–7 MSG

When You Say . . .	God's Word Says
I can't balance everything that is on my plate.	Unless the Lord builds a house, the work of the builders is wasted. Unless the Lord protects a city, guarding it with sentries will do no good. It is useless for you to work so hard from early morning until late at night, anxiously working for food to eat; for God gives rest to his loved ones. Psalm 127:1–5 NLT
I'm exhausted.	Then Jesus said, "Come to me, all of you who are weary and carry heavy burdens, and I will give you rest. Take my yoke upon you. Let me teach you, because I am humble and gentle at heart, and you will find rest for your souls." Matthew 11:28–29 NLT
I don't have the strength to keep going.	Now may our Lord Jesus Christ himself and God our Father, who loved us and by his grace gave us eternal comfort and a wonderful hope, comfort you and strengthen you in every good thing you do and say. 2 Thessalonians 2:16–17 NLT
No one notices all I do.	The eyes of the Lord are on the righteous, and his ears are attentive to their cry. Psalm 34:15
I don't know how to connect with my child.	Show me your ways, Lord, teach me your paths. Guide me in your truth and teach me, for you are God my Savior, and my hope is in you all day long. Psalm 25:4–5
I can't stop worrying about my children.	[He] will keep in perfect peace those whose minds are steadfast, because they trust in [him]. Isaiah 26:3
I'm not making a difference.	He who began a good work in you will carry it on to completion until the day of Christ Jesus. Philippians 1:6

When You Say . . .	God's Word Says
I'm such a bad mom.	And we know that all things work together for good to them that love God, to them who are the called according to his purpose. Romans 8:28 KJV
I can't stop doubting my parenting decisions.	So do not throw away your confidence; it will be richly rewarded. You need to persevere so that when you have done the will of God, you will receive what he has promised. Hebrews 10:35–36
Some days my heart feels hopeless.	We put our hope in the LORD. He is our help and our shield. In him our hearts rejoice, for we trust in his holy name. Let your unfailing love surround us, LORD, for our hope is in you alone. Psalm 33:20–22 NLT
I wish I could know God's plans so I could follow them.	But the plans of the LORD stand firm forever, the purposes of his heart through all generations. Psalm 33:11

mining for gold

24 Traits to Help You Notice and Nurture Character

Be ACCEPTING. Be kind, welcoming, and friendly to others who are different.
"Accept one another, then, just as Christ accepted you"
(Rom. 15:7).

- Listen to others' opinions even if you don't agree with them.
- Get to know someone who has different colored skin than you.
- Stop and talk to or say hi to someone who is disabled.
- Invite a family that is a different ethnicity over for dinner and ask about their culture.

Be ADAPTABLE. Cooperate with changes in people and circumstances.
"Live in harmony with one another" (Rom. 12:16).

- Use what you have instead of complaining about what you don't have.
- Adjust your expectations and work together to resolve conflicts.
- Keep a good attitude when things don't go your way.
- Create a "back-up plan box" with games, cards, crafts, and gift certificates for those unexpected rainy days.

Be CHEERFUL. Have a happy heart.
"A happy heart makes the face cheerful" (Prov. 15:13).
- Choose to be happy even when you don't feel like it.
- Look for reasons to be glad when others are grouchy.
- Smile at strangers.
- Laugh a lot!

Show COMPASSION. Care for others in need.
"The LORD is gracious and compassionate, slow to anger and rich in love" (Ps. 145:8).
- Be kind when someone makes a mistake.
- Don't laugh when someone does something embarrassing.
- Find someone who's lonely and offer to be their friend.
- Show that you care by offering to help when someone is hurting.

Be CONTENT. Be satisfied with what you have.
"Keep your lives free from the love of money and be content with what you have" (Heb. 13:5).
- Don't be jealous of others who have things you want.
- When you start to complain about what you wish you had, make a list of what you do have and tell God thanks for each thing you write down.

- Commit to not buying anything you do not need for one week.
- Start a family gratitude journal. Have each person list three things they are thankful for each day.

Have COURAGE. Be brave even when you are afraid.
"Be strong and courageous . . . for the LORD *your God will be with you wherever you go" (Josh. 1:9).*

- Try something you've never done.
- Ask for help when you feel afraid.
- Push past your fears and do something that shows faith.

Be DILIGENT. Do everything with your best effort.
"Whatever you do, work at it with all your heart" (Col. 3:23).

- Work hard at everything you do.
- Don't let frustrations slow you down.
- Be a team worker and ask others to help you get things done.
- Give it your best shot!

Show FORGIVENESS. Overlook a wrong done to you or someone else.
"Be kind and compassionate to one another, forgiving each other, just as in Christ God forgave you" (Eph. 4:32).

- Don't stay angry when someone hurts your feelings.
- Accept apologies and say, "I forgive you."
- Offer kindness when someone has been unkind to you.

Be GENTLE. Handle someone or something carefully.
"Let your gentleness be evident to all" (Phil. 4:5).

- Hold babies and animals with tenderness and care.
- Be quiet when someone is sleeping nearby.

- Don't throw things inside the house.
- Be careful with things that can break easily.

Be HELPFUL. Do part or all of the work for someone else. *"Not looking to your own interests but each of you to the interests of the others" (Phil. 2:4).*

- Carry all or part of someone else's load.
- Clean up a mess someone else made.
- Offer to help with extra chores at home or at school.
- Unload the dishwasher without being asked.
- Open the door for someone.

Be HONEST. Always tell the truth. *"The LORD detests lying lips, but he delights in people who are trustworthy" (Prov. 12:22).*

- Don't make excuses.
- Confess when you have done something wrong.
- Give something back that isn't yours when you are finished using it.
- Don't blame others for what you did.

Be HOPEFUL. Believe things will work out for the best. *"Faith is confidence in what we hope for and assurance about what we do not see" (Heb. 11:1).*

- Keep a positive outlook even when something seems impossible.
- Look for opportunities beyond the obstacles.
- Believe something good can happen.
- Believe you can do it even when you feel like you can't!

Take INITIATIVE. Do something without being asked.
"Be very careful, then, how you live . . . making the most of every opportunity" (Eph. 5:15–16).

- Do chores or homework without being reminded.
- Offer your time or resources when you see a need.
- Share ideas and suggestions.
- Bring a glass of water to a parent or neighbor doing yardwork.

Use KIND WORDS. Speak words that honor others.
"Gracious words are a honeycomb, sweet to the soul and healing to the bones" (Prov. 16:24).

- Say thanks if someone does something for you or gives something to you.
- Tell others what you like about them.
- Write a note to a friend (or draw a picture) telling them how much you appreciate them.
- Practice saying "please" and "thank you" throughout each mealtime.

Show KINDNESS. Be nice to others.
"Always try to do good to each other and to all people" (1 Thess. 5:15 NLT).

- Let someone in line before you at school or on the playground.
- Be friendly by saying hello and smiling at people.
- Give a thoughtful gift for no reason.
- Befriend someone who doesn't have many friends.

Be OBEDIENT. Do what you are told without questioning. *"Do everything without complaining and arguing" (Phil. 2:14 NLT).*

- Do what your parents and teachers tell you to do.
- Don't argue if you don't like what you are being told to do.
- Follow instructions even when others do not.

Be PATIENT. Wait without complaining. *"Be patient, bearing with one another in love" (Eph. 4:2).*

- Ask for something and then wait without asking again.
- Be patient with yourself when you don't know how to do something.
- Don't interrupt. Wait for your turn to talk.
- Have each family member wait to buy something they really want. See if the desire goes away.

PERSEVERE. Keep trying even when it is hard. *"Let us not become weary in doing good" (Gal. 6:9).*

- Set a goal to learn something new and work at it until you do.
- Give your best effort even if you feel frustrated.
- Don't give up, no matter how hard it gets!

Show RESPECT. Treat others with honor and consideration. *"Show proper respect to everyone" (1 Pet. 2:17).*

- Introduce yourself and shake hands the first time you meet someone.
- Ask permission before using something that doesn't belong to you.
- Look others in the eye when they are talking to you.

Be RESPONSIBLE. Do what is right and be accountable for it.

"Each one should test their own actions. Then they can take pride in themselves" (Gal. 6:4).

- Complete chores and assignments on time.
- Take care of your toys and possessions.
- Follow rules even when no one is looking.

Show SELF-CONTROL. Control your emotions and actions.

"Let us stay awake and be self-controlled" (1 Thess. 5:6 CSB).

- Turn off the television when your set time is over.
- Don't react with anger when someone makes you mad.
- Sit still at the dinner table.

SHARE. Give part of something to someone else.

"Do not forget to do good and to share with others" (Heb. 13:16).

- Share your time by serving someone.
- Share your talents by doing what you do best for someone else to enjoy.
- Share your treasures by letting a friend borrow something of yours.
- Box up toys and clothes that are in good condition to give to a church or other charity.

Be TEACHABLE. Always desire to learn new things.

"Let the wise listen and add to their learning" (Prov. 1:5).

- Be willing to learn from others.
- Try to find out why things work the way they do.
- Look for something new to learn each day.

Be TRUSTWORTHY. Be dependable so others can count on you.

"It is required that those who have been given a trust must prove faithful" (1 Cor. 4:2).

- Keep your promises.
- Be honest and responsible.
- Take care of things you borrow from others.

If you've enjoyed reading A CONFIDENT MOM, *we think you'll love Renee's bestselling book,* A CONFIDENT HEART *(Revell, 2011). Here is an excerpt from the first chapter.*

EXCERPT FROM

a confident heart

Discovering the Shadow of My Doubts

I stood in front of my bathroom mirror, squinting from the bright lights above while also trying to open my eyelids so I could brush mascara on my lashes. My mouth opened too, almost instinctively. I couldn't help but wonder why opening my mouth also opened my eyes. It didn't make sense and neither did the way I was feeling.

My heart was wrestling with self-doubt regarding an event I would be speaking at the next day. I had felt honored, confident, and excited when the leader called months before to invite me to speak at their women's event. Now I questioned whether I should have accepted the invitation in the first place. I couldn't help but wonder, *What's wrong with me?*

I needed to get ready, finish packing my suitcase, and drive to the airport. Instead, I wanted to stay home and do something predictable like fold laundry, order pizza, and watch a movie with my kids. Something less risky than standing in front of five hundred women to give a message that I hoped would challenge and encourage their hearts, bring them laughter, and leave them longing for more of God.

Questions replayed over and over in my head: *What if I completely forget what I am going to say? What if my points aren't that powerful? What if the women don't connect with my stories or laugh at my humor? What if . . . ?*

As I continued to put on my makeup, I asked God—once again—to please take away my uncertainty. I hated feeling this way. Canceling the event wasn't an option. Maybe I could call in sick? No, that wouldn't be good.

This was not the first time I'd struggled with self-doubt. In fact, doubt was something I had dealt with more times than I wanted to recount. As a child I doubted I was worth keeping. My insecurity even kept me from riding the carousel at an amusement park, because I doubted my dad would wait for me. I thought he might leave me forever once I was out of sight.

Doubt also robbed me of the joy of waterskiing as a young girl. I refused to try it because I wasn't sure my family would come back to get me once I let go of the rope. I questioned whether I was good enough in college, so I avoided some great opportunities because they brought the risk of rejection. Even as a young bride, I doubted my husband's faithfulness. Our newlywed memories include a lot of arguments about trust.

Now here I was years later, a grown woman in ministry, doubting myself again. It was getting old. I wondered if perhaps my self-doubt was a sign I was in the wrong calling. I mean, if God calls you to do something, shouldn't you feel confident about it? Shouldn't you want to do it? Shouldn't self-assurance be part of God's equipping?

Maybe you know exactly what I'm talking about. Perhaps you have prayed since you were a little girl to be a mother, and here you are with kids, doubting you have what it takes to be a good mom. Or maybe you've sensed God calling you to serve Him in a way that requires steps of faith, but insecurity has convinced you that you're not smart enough or gifted enough. Perhaps you have wanted to change jobs for a while and now you have the opportunity to do just that, but you don't want to go. The unknown is too scary. Although you've been miserable, at least the misery is familiar where you are now.

I desperately wanted to move out of the shadows of my doubts, but all I could do was go through the motions and pray that God would zap me with confidence. I kept hoping it would happen right there in my bathroom, but it didn't. Doubt and questions continued to criticize me.

Once I finished brushing on my mascara, I turned around to put my makeup bag in my suitcase, which was on the floor behind me. That's when I noticed a huge nine-foot shadow on the wall. I was surprised by how much bigger my shadow was than my five-foot-two-inch frame.

It was distorting my image on the wall by making my body look bigger than it really was. All of a sudden, it dawned on me. My uncertainty had created a huge shadow of doubt. Just like my shadow on the wall was distorting my shape, my doubt was distorting my thoughts and overpowering my emotions with confusion and questions. The shadow of doubt had become bigger than what I doubted—myself.

I just stood there looking at the humongous shadow. Then I bent down to put my makeup bag in my suitcase and sensed God whispering to my heart: *You can only see the shadow because you have turned away from the light. Turn back toward the light.*

As I stood up and turned back toward the light above the mirror, I realized I was no longer standing in the shadow. And that was the day I discovered the shadow of my doubts.

Listening to Doubt's Whispers

In the shadow of doubt, insecurity paralyzes us with statements like:

"I can't do this."

"Things will never change."

"My life isn't going to get better."

"I'll never have the confidence I need."

Those are some depressing thoughts, aren't they? But oh how quickly they weasel their way into our minds and disguise their voices to sound like ours. Sometimes we agree with them and they become our own.

These are the voices of insecurity that cast shadows of doubt over our perspective and keep us from becoming the women we want to be—the women God created us to be. Self-doubt blocks the promise of God's power and truth to change us from the inside out so that we can live with a confident heart.

Have you ever agreed with the whispers of doubt and found yourself living with a sense of discouragement and defeat? Have you felt paralyzed by insecurity, and let it stop you from living confidently? If so, you are not alone.

Maybe, like me, you have wondered why you struggle with self-doubt. Or maybe you've asked God to take away your in-securities and give you a more confident personality, yet you are still waiting for that to happen. Perhaps you are good at hiding your doubts and no one but you knows the paralyzing power they have on your life.

As you read the title of this book, did any hint of doubt creep in to tell you it's not possible to have a confident heart? It wouldn't surprise me. Doubt keeps us from believing things can get better. Doubt convinces us that it's not worth the effort. Doubt shouts from the sidelines:

"It's too hard."

"You might as well quit."

"Go ahead and give up. Just close the book now and walk away."

It's Not Supposed to Be This Way

Don't listen to those thoughts, my friend. God doesn't want us stuck in a cycle of defeat or living in the shadows of doubt. He reminds us in Isaiah 49:23, "Then you will know that I am the LORD; those who hope in me will not be disappointed." Yet, doubt and hope cannot live in our hearts at the same time. As God's girls, we need to know and believe that change is possible. We need to hope that life can be different. Otherwise, doubt will win every time and our hearts will be eroded by attitudes and emotions of defeat—but it is not supposed to be this way.

God declares with confidence that things can change—"See, I am doing a new thing!" "I am working all things together for good, because you love me and are called according to my purpose." "All things are possible for [she] who believes" (Isa. 43:19; Rom. 8:28; Mark 9:23 NASB).

Over the past few years, I've found lasting confidence by living daily in the security of God's promises. He's led me beyond believing *in Him* to really *believing Him* by relying on the power of His Words and living like they are true no matter what my feelings tell me. Some days I do better than others, and you will too. But I've found that when I choose to dwell in the assurance of whose I am and who I am in Him, I have a confident heart.

The God of all hope is calling you out of the shadow of your doubts so you can live with a confident heart! Are you ready to let His Word change the way you think, which will determine the way you feel and eventually transform the way you live (Rom. 12:2)? This will be a process that happens if you are willing to have honest, soul-searching conversations with God, yourself, and a few people you trust—conversations about where you are, how you got here, and where you really long to be.

If you are looking for a friend you can trust with the things of your heart, this book is a great place to start. We'll learn how to live beyond the shadows of self-doubt by holding each of our insecurities up to the light of God's Word. We'll talk about the struggles, uncertainty, and fears we all face and how we can learn to actively trust God's heart as we process our never-ending thoughts, our always-changing emotions, and our oh-so-busy and often confusing lives through the transforming truth of God's Word. And we will find our heart's confidence in Christ as we learn how to rely on the power of His promises in our everyday lives.

Are you ready to take God's hand and trust His heart? If so, let's get started together in prayer.

Praying God's Promises

Lord, I pray that You would give me a confident heart in Christ. Take me beyond believing in You to truly believing You. Help me rely on the power of Your promises and live like they are true. You say blessed is the one who trusts in You and whose hope and confidence are found in You. Those who hope in You will not be disappointed, because You work all things together for good for those who love You and are called according to Your purpose. Amen.

See Jeremiah 17:7; Isaiah 49:23; Romans 8:28

acknowledgments

J.J., there aren't enough words to describe the ways you have loved, served, and encouraged me the past few years, especially during my long days and nights of writing. You are the love of my life and my very best friend!

Joshua, Andrew, Aster, Brandi, and Hannah Rose, every one of my favorite memories includes you. Let's make a thousand more together!

Leah and Lynn, your friendship, love, encouragement, prayers, and lunch dates are sweet gifts to my soul. I love you both with all my heart.

MaryAnn, your prayers, encouragement, and lifelong friendship have helped me become all Jesus created me to be as a wife, mom, and leader—but especially as a writer and communicator of His hope and love.

Cammie, Rachel, Callie, Krista, Alex, Kristin, Nancy, Holley, Kristen, Jennifer, Anjuli, K.J., Patrice, Niki, Jen, Cindy, Michele, Mycah, Lucretia, Jenny, Jordan, Sumer, Lindsey, Stephanie, Lara, and Gretchen: thank you for praying over me, my family, and these words throughout the past two years. I don't know that I could've finished without the power of your love, prayers, and encouragement!

Lysa, thank you for inviting me to be part of Proverbs 31 Ministries and for entrusting me to review your article that included the story God used so powerfully in my journey as a mom. Months later, when you asked me to speak in your place at the Calvary MOPS group and share my story, along with my Mining for Gold character chart, it was those moms' smiles and tears that told me I wasn't the only one who needed this message. God has used you in countless ways in my life, and I'm forever grateful.

Barbara Wilson, Marilynn Chadwick, and Lara Kasay, God used you in more ways than you will ever know to influence my legacy as a mom. I am so grateful for the times I had a front-row seat to watch the way you enjoyed motherhood and how you intentionally shepherded the hearts of your children. Whether we were in your home or in the hallways at church, on the playground at McDonald's, or on our knees in prayer, God used you to shape some of the best parts of me.

Andrea Doering, my incredible gift-from-God editor, thank you for EVERYTHING! And to the whole team at Revell—editorial, marketing, and design—I am so grateful for your gifts and that I get to be on the same team with each of you!

Most of all, Jesus, thank You for all the ways You love me. You were there for me in such a personal way that day I wanted to quit, and You spoke to my heart in the most creative, tender, and insightful ways. Everything changed that day because of You. Thank You for giving me a new place to start at the cross of Calvary, and again and again in the ordinary everyday grace You shower over me.

Chapter 1 The Day I Almost Quit

1. Zig Ziglar, *Raising Positive Kids in a Negative World* (New York: Ballantine, 1985), 51.
2. Ziglar, *Raising Positive Kids*.
3. Renee Swope, *A Confident Heart* (Grand Rapids: Revell, 2011), 119–20.

Chapter 3 Reorienting Your Heart to the Goodness of God

1. John Ortberg, *The Life You've Always Wanted* (Grand Rapids: Zondervan, 1997), 41.

Chapter 7 Your Child Needs to Know Character Matters Most

1. Henry Cloud and John Townsend, *Raising Great Kids* (Grand Rapids: Zondervan, 1999), 29.
2. Cloud and Townsend, *Raising Great Kids*.

Chapter 10 Your Child Needs to Feel Your Acceptance and Approval

1. Max Lucado, *You Are Special*, illustrated ed. (Wheaton: Crossway, 2000).

Chapter 11 Your Child Needs to Feel Known and Understood

1. Florence Littauer, *Personality Plus for Parents* (Grand Rapids: Revell, 2000), 16–19.
2. Littauer, *Personality Plus for Parents*, 37.

Chapter 12 Your Child Needs to Feel Loved and Pursued

1. Gary Chapman and Ross Campbell, *The 5 Love Languages of Children* (Chicago: Northfield, 2016), 22.
2. Chapman and Campbell, *5 Love Languages of Children*, 111.

Chapter 14 Your Child Needs to Know the Power of Prayer

1. Renee Swope, *A Confident Heart Devotional* (Grand Rapids: Revell, 2013), 59.
2. "Praying Circles Around the Lives of Your Children," Mark Batterson, accessed March 29, 2021, https://www.markbatterson.com/books/praying-circles-around-the-lives-of-your-children/.

Chapter 23 You Can Do Hard Things

1. Lysa TerKeurst, *The Best Yes* (Nashville: Thomas Nelson, 2014), 175.

Chapter 27 Guilt Is Stealing Time You Don't Have to Lose

1. Laura Tremaine, https://www.lauratremaine.com/.

Chapter 28 God Loves You and Wants to Be with You

1. Renee Swope, *A Confident Heart* (Grand Rapids: Revell, 2011), 36.

Chapter 29 You've Got What It Takes to Be a Confident Mom

1. "Site of the First Documented Discovery of Gold in the United States," North Carolina Historic Sites, accessed March 16, 2021, https://historicsites.nc.gov/all-sites/reed-gold-mine/history.
2. Emily Ley, *Grace Not Perfection* (Nashville: Thomas Nelson, 2019), 215, 217–18.

RENEE SWOPE and her husband, J.J., have been married for twenty-eight years, and they love spending time together with their family in the mountains or on the lake. Renee is an Enneagram 7w6 who loves adventure and beauty! When she's not writing or recording podcasts, you will find Renee having coffee with a friend, DIYing a home remodeling project, doing landscape gardening, or hosting guests at their family's Airbnb.

Renee is also the international bestselling author of *A Confident Heart* and host of her *A Confident Mom* podcast. She is a contributing writer for (in)courage, a division of DaySpring, and served in leadership at Proverbs 31 Ministries for twenty years as radio cohost and executive director. Renee and her family love calling North Carolina home.

JOIN RENEE

for personal encouragement
to help you live a confident life!

Visit ReneeSwope.com

to download free resources and watch videos to enhance your personal study, share with your small group, or contribute to your book club. You can also see Renee's speaking schedule or join the next *A Confident Heart* online study.

f A Confident Heart by Renee Swope
f Renee Swope y ReneeSwope □ ReneeSwope

More Resources from Renee

A Confident Mom Podcast
reneeswope.com/a-confident-mom/podcast

And Additional Resources:

24 Character Trait Cards
reneeswope.com/mining-for-gold
Password: gomom

Scripture Prayers for Parents
reneeswope.com/scripture-prayers-for-parents

A Confident Mom Online Community
reneeswope.com/a-confident-mom/community

A Confident Mom Mini-Course
reneeswope.com/a-confident-mom/mini-course

Confident, Strong, and Free — You're Closer Than You Think

Ever feel like you're not good enough, smart enough, or valuable enough? Renee Swope understands. Even with a great family, a successful career, and a thriving ministry, she still struggled with self-doubt. In *A Confident Heart* and *A Confident Heart Devotional*, Renee shares her journey and gives you the keys to stepping toward the life of faith God designed for you.